library cards explains to me, once you've chosen a username, a so-called alias, it lasts forever. Panzerdivision.

It's the same with this nickname as with the past itself: everyone knows you can't run away from it. And it seems to be true: you can move, like I did, to a foreign country, settle there, learn to speak and write the language so that, sometimes at least, people mistake you for one of the locals. You think you can disappear. But regardless of where you go and how long you've lived in a foreign country: everyone there already saw your Wanted poster. And they're laughing or snarling at you: Panzerdivision!

So the username remains in place. And in the end I can't rule out the possibility that the book I want to dedicate to my great-grandfather will sooner or later be invaded by Germans.

I'm going to start by also giving him a kind of nickname or username, since I don't want to constantly be writing 'my great-grandfather', which after all isn't his most important role in life, nor his full name, Florens Christian Rang, nor Florens Christian, which is what I always heard from my father's side of the family, where he's treated with respectful familiarity. Let alone 'our hero', which I don't like in either an ironic or an actual sense. FCR (like JFK) would be concise and practical, but definitely makes you think too readily of a football club. So, what username would I choose if I had to apply for a Bibliothèque nationale card for him today? Plenty of words would apply to him: seeker, maniac, radical, malcontent, rebel. But what I'm looking for is a name,

It begins with my username, which is 'Panzerdivision'. I chose it years ago, when I first applied for a card to access the lower level of the Bibliothèque nationale, open only to researchers. To reserve a seat and to order books online you need a pseudonym. I could of course have chosen something like 'nasturtium' or 'silkworm'. I had chosen 'Panzerdivision'. That was the nickname once bestowed upon me by an exceptionally charming Frenchman who was second to none in the refined art of irony, an art that has more recently fallen in my estimation. It should be pronounced as nasally as possible, with a soft S and the stress on the final syllable: Pansèredivisión. At the time, this nickname, which I had earned not only because I am German but also because of certain personal traits that were and presumably still are typical of me, struck me as funny. In the context of the research I plan to carry out with the aid of this username, it no longer sounds so funny. The focus of that research will be a German who spent some years in Poland. My great-grandfather.

To make it clear from the outset: my great-grandfather didn't invade Poland. The region around Poznań where he lived had been annexed by Prussia as early as 1815.

Still. I'd like to change my library pseudonym. It's not possible. As the grumpy woman in charge of issuing a password. I choose – after a bird I've often seen on the French coast, running back and forth following the surf – the name Sanderling.

The first thing that endeared this man to me once he began to monopolize my attention was the title of his unpublished, never-completed major work, which has survived only in fragments. The book was going to be called *Reckoning with God*, and it would consist primarily of a comprehensive history and critique of Christianity along with an outline of a future religion, illustrated or rather substantiated through an account of his own spiritual journey.

Reckoning with God: he was serious about this title, as he was about everything he took on in life. And what about me? I give it some thought. Yes, I'm also serious, more and more so in fact, though no doubt my seriousness is different in kind from Sanderling's. Time, however, is not serious. *Reckoning with God*: all it took was the time shift into the twenty-first century for the title to lose some of its seriousness. Without any intervention on my part, merely through the passage of time, the title has become comical. Seriousness of the kind that was still widespread in Sanderling's day has disappeared from our world, or at least from our immediate, trusted circles. But maybe not altogether?

The delusions of grandeur behind that deadly serious title leave you speechless. In my mind I see a small man – I imagine him being short, not for his time but for ours – though an additional twenty or even thirty centimetres would have made no difference to his minuteness in the presence of Him with whom he wished to reach a reckoning. Thus I picture him, a small man, all on his own, his fists raised towards the heavens and yelling out his fury with body and soul; I see him, this is how he himself describes it, tearing his hat from his head and stamping on it as he screams into the *vast forests: you swine, you scoundrel*, and again and again *swine, scoundrel*, and he means *God the tormentor, the 'father' who from on high inflicted this upon me*. I hear how his words are swallowed at a height of only a few metres by a mute, not even scornful infinity.

Sanderling believed that someone, that is, a God, was engaged with him personally; he did not yet have the feeling of disappearing within a confusing mass. Who inflicted this *upon me*! Like Job he felt he'd been dealt with most unjustly, yet what did the misfortune look like into which he'd been undeservedly thrust? Had he, like Job, lost his wife, his ten children and all of his possessions, had he like Job been smitten with sore boils from the sole of his foot unto his crown? What exactly had been done to him? It's not at all clear whether that's something we'll still be able to find out over a hundred years later.

Reckoning with God: we're dealing with someone who wasn't going to be intimidated, it seems. Or are we dealing with someone who consumed too much Nietzsche? Possibly both. I want to explore the seriousness and the delusions of grandeur with which, a hundred years ago, those words were noted down and double-underlined.

Instead of being stuck, like his great-granddaughter was, with a common or garden name, this serious fellow bore a name that almost amounts to an ethos: Rang. According to the Brothers Grimm's dictionary, the German word Rang designates the level a person occupies within a social order; it presumes hierarchy. I'd imagine that someone called Rang would have to feel different from a person called Fisher, Weber or Smith. Would it ever occur to a person with the name Rang that the level in question might be the lowest, the last? But of course these reflections don't reveal anything besides my own prejudice. Presumably a Herr Groß doesn't feel much different from a Herr Klein.

What about Magnus, though? In the Rang family, several oil paintings of ancestors are passed down from generation to generation, always to the eldest son, including a canvas depicting one Magnus Rang. This Magnus bears a certain resemblance to Louis XIV, due no doubt to the powdered wig, a so-called allonge, whose white coils surround his head like hair in curlers, and to the double chin. I imagine that someone who's called Magnus feels differently about himself than a Kurt or a John does, and I think I'm correct about that.

The Rang we're going to be dealing with here was given the first name Christian. In later years, when he had grown weary of Christianity as it was practised by the churches of his time, he adopted a second name, one that from the viewpoint of today, and perhaps also of his own day, seems pretentious, a name that wasn't calculated to demote its bearer within the rankings: Florens. He who flourishes. Christianity appeared to him, all of a sudden, withered and arid. He thrust it away and blossomed. Florens Christian Rang.

It's a long way from Florens to Panzerdivision. That route, paved with words, is the one this book will travel along, moving forwards and backwards, except when it takes detours or goes down side roads.

And here, right at the beginning, before we've even got started with the great-grandfather – this book won't suit impatient readers – comes the first stop: the word Boche, or Bosch.

You should definitely apply for a Crossing Borders grant from the Robert Bosch Foundation, someone says when I tell them about my plan to follow in Sanderling's footsteps to Poland. I'm not at all surprised to find out about a grant that seems tailor-made for me: it's well known that in Germany there's financial support for just about any project you can imagine. Why not, if it's tailor-made for you, I say to myself. And then in the next second: do you really need this money? Can't you travel to Poland without outside support? It will mean you'll have to thank the Bosch Foundation in the book's acknowledgements, advertising for the Bosch company. Proudly refusing such funding would, it seems to me, be honourable. While I'm still pondering this, wavering between honour and money, I realize I've already set off on my journey and find myself halfway between Florens and Panzerdivision, between Sanderling and myself.

'Boche' is one of the most common insults French people apply to Germans; these days it's often used as if in quotation marks, and in rare cases like this, the irony serves to soften instead of heightening the nastiness. Because the word is pronounced exactly the same as the name of the German firm Bosch, for years I assumed that was where it came from. Since someone pointed out my mistake, I looked into it, and indeed: it seems to be nothing more than an odd coincidence that the two words are homonyms. So where does the insulting term come from? Supposedly from alboche, a contraction of allemand and caboche, meaning more or less 'German pighead'. That sounds like a friendly pleonasm; friendlier in any case than the word Boche does when you get it thrown at your own pighead. Less friendly, however, than the word rigolboche, which also exists in French and which means 'a barrel of laughs', in other words the opposite of a German. I've taken the etymology of the word Boche from the *Trésor de la langue française*, and I'll do my best to believe it. But does this mean it was completely absurd to have spent years associating the Bosch firm with the insult 'Boche'?

What you can find out about Bosch is full of contradictions. Let's take that as a sign that this book's journey will be paved with almost as many contradictions as words. Some regard the company's founder, Robert Bosch, as an admirable saviour of human lives, even as someone who committed himself to a form of political resistance. The common good, in particular the health of his fellow human beings, mattered a great deal to him; among other things, he had a hospital built in Stuttgart. On the other hand, Hitler ordered that Robert Bosch be given a state funeral. And above all: more than half the workers at the Dreilinden Maschinenbau firm, a subsidiary of Bosch that mostly supplied the German Luftwaffe, were forced labourers, prisoners of war and concentration camp internees who had been deported to the Kleinmachnow satellite camp. Dreilinden is a neighbourhood of Kleinmachnow, where the subsidiary was based. On the one hand, on the other hand? What appears indisputable is that the company directors were not enthusiastic Nazis, but to avoid expropriation they reached an agreement with the regime. And that the company profited handsomely from the war instigated by that regime.

So: do I want money from Bosch?

I decide to submit an application, if only because doing so will immediately get me under way with the book. If I'm offered the funding, I tell myself in provisional self-defence, I could still turn it down with a demonstrative, theatrical gesture: me, take money from you? Never! Or my application will be declined and I'll avoid any moral dilemma. Let's wait and see.

It's a short distance from the Bosch or Boche station to another, where I'll stop off before turning to Sanderling. The word that imposes itself on me is one he may never have heard. With which he would have had no associations. In his day it didn't have any particular significance. It's a word I myself have heard and read hundreds, no, thousands of times, but that I've almost never uttered. And even now I'm not going to pronounce it, only write it down. It's not the only word that creates a void around itself, by no means the only one that won't pass my lips. In this case, however, that not wanting to pass my lips is not a figure of speech but a commandment I feel keenly: the word doesn't want to be spoken by me. I don't know if it ever wants to be spoken out loud, and if it does, how and by whom. It's the name of a place in Poland, a place name that by now everyone will have understood.

Some time ago I listened to a programme on French radio during which the word was spoken. That in itself isn't unusual; on the contrary. As I said earlier, it's a word you often hear, which demonstrates that others don't feel the same uneasiness about it as I do. On the programme in question, it was the host who mentioned the word almost in passing. Like all French people, she pronounced the 'Au' like 'O'. And as I've been taken aback to hear a few other times from French speakers, she shifted the 'sch' to the end of the word. So she uttered a word that sounded more or less like 'Oswitsch'. The programme did not, incidentally, focus on what that word will henceforth be associated with, but rather on poetry, and the word only came up in connection with a question that's become a set phrase: 'Can you still write poetry after A.?' But perhaps my memory is deceiving me there.

It isn't deceiving me regarding how the rest of the programme went. Several months have passed since it was broadcast, and I haven't stopped thinking about it. Among the guests on the programme was a French Jew. She was the first person to talk after *the word* had been spoken. With a voice whose sharpness imprinted itself on my memory, she asked the host – though this request sounded more like a reprimand, even a command – never again to speak the word the way she had just done, and she demonstrated how to pronounce it properly. The pronunciation she found fault with, which she called incorrect, seemed in her eyes to express impermissible negligence and insufficient respect for the word and what it stands for. She didn't actually say that, but you could tell it was what she meant from her irritated, hostile tone. The host apologized then carried on with what she was saying, apparently unaffected.

As I try now, by writing about it, to get to the bottom of what went through my mind at the time and since then, on the one hand I have a clear feeling of how carefully I must choose my words, while on the other I'm aware, as I was then, of my contradictory perception of this incident. It seems to me that this tiny incident, which lasted only a few seconds, reflected all the difficulties and complexities of the relationship between Jews and non-Jews since – then.

I understood this woman striking a brusque tone; she obviously couldn't tolerate a pronunciation she experienced as careless and wrong. At the same time I felt some resistance to this reprimand. Although I almost never utter the word in question, I felt as if the rebuke had been directed at me personally. My vague feeling was and is that as a non-Jew, and moreover as a German, even if I try hard, I simply *can't* pronounce the word correctly. Is that perhaps one of the reasons I avoid doing so?

Later I reflect on what 'correct' and 'wrong' even mean in this context. What the French Jew on the radio programme regarded as correct was, as she herself no doubt knew better than anyone, the pronunciation that's common in French of the German form of the Polish place name Oświęcim. Considered objectively like that, her annoyance over the incorrect or to her intolerable pronunciation of the word doesn't seem justified. Her reaction wasn't a matter of reason, though, but rather one that resulted from indistinct and varying feelings, and the word in question and everything it contains are more than sufficient justification for such a reaction. It is also, however, a reaction that we (and by that 'we' I mean non-Jews and above all German non-Jews) must always be prepared for and to which we can make no objection. We are forbidden from responding to it with feelings; yet what is even more 'verboten' for us is to reply in a neutral and detached manner. I'm not, however, writing all this to complain about something or somebody, and certainly not to represent me or 'us' as pitiable, but to at least once in my life get closer to the open wound that until now I've always tried to avoid.

So what would the 'correct' pronunciation of the word have been? Probably the Polish pronunciation with as little accent as possible, even if hardly anyone besides

Poles themselves would know what that ought to sound like. I discover that you don't necessarily need to know a Polish person you can ask; you can easily find out on the internet. All you need to do is type in the word itself and 'pronunciation'. On my screen, a large black window opens. Maybe that same black window, as if looking out on a starless night, would have opened up if I'd wanted to know how to pronounce the word krzesło (chair) or dziękuję (thank you). I didn't try it. I know what the windows that open up in the digital world otherwise look like: they're filled with images, no space is free of images or text, and those images and sometimes also that text are in constant motion. But the window I'm talking about is inert, and uniformly black. The only thing to be seen is a narrow grey strip in the centre, on the left next to it an arrow, and on the right the digits 0:01 and a loudspeaker symbol. I click on the arrow and hear a man's voice saying the word in Polish. It's not a droning automated voice as I expected, but the serious, warm voice of a man. I listen to the word over and over, quietly at first then a little louder. What I hear could be phonetically rendered approximately as Oschwientschim. It sounds as if that would be the correct pronunciation, albeit not one that could be used in conversation.

Why such a long passage about this word and its pronunciation at the beginning of a book that's supposed to be about my great-grandfather who died in 1924?

I think of the time that separates the two of us as being like a path. We're two walkers on different stretches of the same route who never encounter each other. The part that extends from his death to my birth, which neither of us will ever set foot on, is at once what unites and separates us. If I now ready myself, equipped with all kinds of insights about the circumstances of this special life, and more generally about his time and some of the prevailing intellectual trends and attitudes, to travel that section of the path, I can't simply jump over the connecting and separating link and act as if there was nothing in between, as if I wasn't the great-granddaughter but rather the daughter of this man.

As I search for a possible approach to this distant life, I therefore decide to concentrate on the turn of the century and to the years he spent in the east, in Poznań, which was then a Prussian city known as Posen, and later in two villages in the surrounding area. For if a single word could capture what unites and at the same time separates us, would it not be the aforementioned one I so stubbornly avoided, or indeed that other word associated with it: Poland?

If I were to meet Sanderling today, in an afterlife conjured up by me or by someone else – and what is the past if not an inaccessible realm of the dead? – and he asked me what had happened in the world that used to be his since he left, would I not first of all have to pronounce the dreaded word?

All these associations probably go without saying and don't need to be expressly mentioned. Yet like all things that go without saying, they melt into thin air if they aren't occasionally thought and deeply felt by somebody and thus severed from their self-evident quality.

As a living being, as a memory of a living person, Sanderling has disappeared from the minds of those alive today. The last people who knew him died in the 1970s, and I never talked with any of them. However, what remains of him amounts to infinitely more than you can draw on for most people who died a long time ago. There's an extensive estate that's stored in an archive in ideal conditions; there are published and unpublished writings and correspondence; there are some descriptions of what he was like as a person, including those penned by Walter Benjamin and Hofmannsthal. There are photographs. There are the places where he lived.

Today I'm still unfamiliar with most of that material. My journey into the past will lead through a vast quantity of papers, places and encounters. That will be the journey of this book. It will narrate not only people and events, intellectual and spiritual movements, but also the thickets of history. It will be the journal of a trip of exploration.

A secret surrounds the personality of this man, something that seems to have revealed itself to everyone who met him yet which upon his death was probably closed off forever. Something that is even harder to grasp for those who never met him. Does the written word, for which he felt such great reverence, become a dead letter when it tries to capture him? Might it be possible to bring that dead letter to life?

Let's try it out with a short, simple sentence. Let's say: he's a well-behaved little boy. But no, even that isn't right. A child is well behaved out of fear of being punished or simply because they don't feel any need to do what isn't allowed. Neither of those is the case with Sanderling as a child. If we wish to believe him, and I do, when he violated prohibitions, as he did frequently, he didn't fear punishment, didn't fear the pain of being given a beating, but feared being *exposed as someone who recognized the sanctity of the prohibition yet nonetheless violated it*. Parents are higher beings whose will must be obeyed. The boy already contains within him the man who, as he would be described later, was endowed with an aura and inspired respect. He himself calls this being *passively authoritarian*. The authority is embedded in him but at first can only express itself passively, that's to say via its opposite, obedience: *I was subordinate to my parents to an extreme degree.*

Does that subordination contain something of the so-called 'blind' obedience we're accustomed to blaming for the worst crimes? By *we* I mean those of us who would never have thought of rebelling against God. For whom God is a similarly bygone figure or institution as the German Kaiser. Those of us for whom there's never been any authority.

So what about this boy's obedience?

In the mass of notes, writings and statements with the aid of which I'm attempting to draw near to this past life, every now and then a word or phrase or piece of information stands out, something that has, or that I give, particular meaning. For example, it's mentioned in passing that Sanderling's father had the boy, born in 1864, baptized as a Catholic but educated in the Protestant religion, as a protest against the dogma of papal infallibility that had been proclaimed during the First Vatican Council. Anyone who publicly doubted the infallibility of the Pope was literally threatened with excommunication. But here was a man who only recognized a single infallible being, and that was God Himself. He refused to have his son brought up in the belief that a human being could be infallible, even if only in the restricted realms of religious and moral questions. And besides (I'm adding this myself), how much value is there in an infallibility that first has to be voted on? And that, once the bishops have voted in favour of it, you have to proclaim yourself? Couldn't any old person come along and claim this?

I want to see my forefather's refusal to recognize the Pope as infallible and his rejection of this new dogma – even if he didn't do it officially and there was no excommunication – as defiance that is incompatible with thoughtless obedience. He knew that neither the Pope as head of the Church nor he himself as head of his family could be infallible. If he nevertheless demanded complete subordination from his young son, that may have simply been because he regarded himself for the time being as more reasonable and experienced.

'Defiance' is no doubt the wrong term. But this much appears to be right: this man didn't simply swallow everything. He had a mind of his own. He mistrusted anyone who wished his personal decisions to be regarded as absolute and not open to question. When I think about what came later (so for me, what came earlier), and I think about that a lot these days, it reassures me to be able to write that about one of my forebears.

His son, my great-grandfather, is thus authoritarian in a sense that is no longer current today; the word has come above all to evoke military dictatorship. Indeed, according to the most recent dictionaries, it's more or less synonymous with totalitarian. Sanderling is authoritarian at a time when a suit of armour still had a human being inside it. At first he is passively authoritarian; later, with his own children and probably those subordinate to him, perhaps also with his wife, actively so.

The future takes shape within him in the form of opposites: order and anarchy, hesitation and precipitousness, obedience and rebellion, ideals and reality.

Father and Mother were idealists too, but in a very different way to me. Optimists, so to speak: they had domestic, moral, social ideals that they fulfilled and wanted to see fulfilled. My idealism could not be fulfilled, I was by nature disorderly. Dreams of a vague beyond went against my parents' way of being.

Anyone who is and wishes to remain an optimist is best advised to find ideals that can be fulfilled. An ideal you can fulfil is in itself a contradiction. His parents had a precise notion of how a person ought to behave.

For Sanderling, the ideal is something floating, an ethereal form, and thus by definition unattainable. The essential had always, in his eyes, taken place outside the sphere of the visible, in a misty landscape with sunlight breaking through clouds, a place that didn't in any way resemble his parents' neat, orderly living room. When the mist disperses and the reality of things, people and conditions becomes visible, optimism is difficult to accomplish.

Optimists, idealists, authority, ideals – are any of the words from that not-so-distant time still holding out? Books about the past employ the words in common use at that time, and what other words could they choose? But it's as if someone had pulled the rug out from under their feet. And it's not only abstract terms that have drifted away. Won't 'street', 'school', 'letter' also soon be out of view? We move forwards on wobbly legs.

Poland and the role of pastor are still a long way off. The child, the young man, has received *the inheritance of a career as a public official*. Another term that's barely recognizable any more: official. Does anyone still come from a *long line of officials*? No doubt some people do, beginning with me, since I represent the first generation of non-officials in the Rang genealogy. But no one any longer seriously considers it a heritage to be taken up. Time was when for better German families a career as a public official represented the same as the priesthood and the military did for French nobility: a status to which a son was dispatched. Sanderling's father and he himself ended their careers having, like Goethe, attained the title of Geheimer Rat, or Privy Councillor.

The last century has robbed the profession of public official not only of all its prestige, but also of any sense of vocation. Little of that remains: just an increasingly shabby shelter for anxious souls who hope for job security, treatment by the best doctors and a decent pension. What caused the public official to fall from the firmament and finally from its pedestal?

Hard though it may be for us to believe, when the young Sanderling embraces this career, there's still a religious dimension to everything, including administration. This is a profession whose spiritual aspect has been gradually draining away. Sanderling sees the beginning of this development, and regards it as an *immensely significant problem in world history: the replacement of religion by dispassionate administration* through *illiberal, uninspired detachment.*

In a book entitled *Der verwaltete Mensch* (Administered Man), H.G. Adler describes administration as a reflection of social reality: 'Strictly speaking, administration doesn't say anything, it only writes' (a radical variant of realist literature that aims to depict reality as faithfully as possible?). The human being appears in administration as a process, as an abstraction. As a number.

Adler explains how originally administration, in service to the three state powers, leads a parallel existence revolving around accounting, until under National Socialism it becomes a power itself, no longer merely concerning itself with people's lives but affecting them.

Within administration, however, its masters, and at the same time its servants, are the officials. An army of officials – no less obedient than a regiment of soldiers – sorted, administered, calculated, pushed columns of figures to the east. Categorized them.

'No state has ever been administered more like a factory than Prussia since the death of Frederick William I.' Adler quotes this sentence by Novalis from the Grimms' dictionary, where it's supposed to elucidate the etymology of the word verwalten (administer). It may read like a dark prophecy, but it presumably was only intended as a critique of Frederick II's regime.

We're seeing words get away from us. We can't catch up with any of them; no sentence can any longer be understood the way it was meant and only that way. You would have to forget – no, we know how it goes with what's forgotten, that it has by no means disappeared but instead is lying there crumpled up behind the carefully ironed sheets in the airing cupboard – and you would have to delete a whole century. Come into the world a hundred years earlier. In 1864. You'd have to be your own great-grandfather. Florens Christian Rang.

From generation to generation, men in this family, in this *lineage*, became highly ranked officials, an honourable career yet even then one not well suited to those of passionate temperament. And Sanderling had a passionate, hot-blooded temperament; much about him is uncertain, but that much can be said with confidence. Yet he's a compliant, deferential son, and so he doesn't reject the inheritance of this career and does embark on the required study of law. What follow are some years which do not pass by in a flash as this account might suggest. What engages his attention is not the law. It's – but how am I, how is *anyone* supposed to know that. I was going to write: it's the warm and marvellously tender skin of women. Abruptly, his gaze meets mine from very close, and it's as if I'm standing face to face with a living person. He forbids me from making any mention of his physical existence. He forbids me from getting closer to him in any way. He would rather continue to vegetate away, incognito, in the shadow of Benjamin and Buber than be dragged into the diffuse light of the world of my imagination. He doesn't acknowledge me as his greatgranddaughter. He never wanted to have one like me. And I can't help but think, at this moment, of my birth certificate, on which is written 'Paternity indicated in a marginal note'.

I stand up straight and look into his light, luminous eyes. I'm your last chance, I say in a firm voice. Apart from me and an Italian doctoral student who would need a grant to carry out his research, a grant he won't receive, not one person is interested in you any more. You footnote, I shout at him. You're nothing but a marginal note!

In my own imagination, at least, I like to allow myself now and then to put on this kind of powerful performance.

But how to go on?

Others can write sentences like 'He must have been driven by strong erotic and aggressive impulses' or 'He became sexually active, lived beyond his means, and was continually overcome by feelings of guilt.' I'm sticking with it: what affects him most deeply, what won't relinquish its hold on him, is the warm and marvellously tender skin of women.

He reads Schopenhauer and Gerhart Hauptmann, goes to the theatre.

Some of the work makes him feel carried away; being carried away is what he longs for more than anything, and he has a distinct talent for it.

But girls and women carry him outside of himself. The feelings of depravity and guilt overwhelm him. It's easy to write something like that, and everyone believes they understand it, everyone knows that until recently it was bad for men and women to lie together unless they were married. But how can I, for whom time has long since removed that weight, comprehend the feeling of guilt and the way it burdened each individual? Is it as if I felt an irrepressible urge to torture others, to inflict physical pain upon them, and couldn't stop myself, even though I knew how awful it was and even though I hated myself for doing it?

Such comparisons can never be fair; perhaps they can help in the attempt – which we must make even as we know it can't possibly succeed – to catapult ourselves a hundred years back in time. He feels like a leper, I think, like someone possessed by a demon he's too weak to fight back against. And he despises himself for it.

There's a wild animal living inside him. He can tame it to some degree, but he can't rid himself of it.

In carrying out my design, I didn't have the courage to risk approaching any of the beautiful, proud apparitions, and the creature I enticed, and took into my bed twice a week, had only one arm. The other was a sheath made by a bandagist... Nothing kept me with her besides my lack of courage, which meant I didn't want to hurt the docile thing's feelings by sending her away, and my need not to passively succumb to my wild imaginings... So now I cut a piece of paper into a cross and attached it to the wall over my bed. When the sweet girl came, I took it down; I did the same thing when someone came to visit.

Academic researchers may one day uncover more about this man as an intellectual. I'm heir to the other man, who's lying there next to a girl with one arm. And I'm pleased about that, because what emerges from those lines is a human being, one for whom I'm beginning to feel affection.

There's no posturing in his narrative, and nor does he spare himself. Am I supposed to be indignant because he's ashamed of the one-armed girl, because he's not familiar with the law requiring that disabled people be treated equally, because he feels pity for her instead of seeing her as his *equal*? More than anything, he's ashamed of himself for not loving this girl, for using her and presumably closing his eyes as he does so.

I can imagine, a hundred years from now, a descendant of mine or some other self-important so-and-so poking their nose into my papers, scouring the notes I've left behind for anything untoward and using their future criteria and certainties to understand and judge me. Shaping my hands into a funnel around my mouth, I shout at this fool to – but no, they're sitting in their futuristic glass house with a pile of stones to hand and can't hear me.

The paper cross pulls at my heartstrings. He could have nailed a simple wooden cross over his bed or one forged out of metal, which would have been just as easy to take down. The paper cross demonstrates the consistency of his faith and of his inner commandments during those years. And that he held on to them, in spite of everything. That wafer-thin God, light as a feather, weighed so heavily on his heart that when the one-armed girl knocked at his door – twice a week, at set times – he couldn't stand having Him within his sight. Perhaps that God even weighed all the more heavily, the lighter and more crumpled He felt between his fingers.

The girl didn't undress. She came and remained the way she was, with her arm of wrapped cloth, a doll you could turn around and hold against yourself. Did she receive something in exchange? Certainly not money. But perhaps a certain amount of respect, or even affection? Otherwise why would he have worried about hurting her feelings if he told her to stop coming to see him?

These regular rendezvous don't have any of the paper lightness of that cross, and even less of the frivolous and joyful feeling of a lovers' tryst. They are black vortexes, dark holes in the week, fists pressed into eye sockets behind which lightning sweeps across the landscape and the strokes of a whip lash the guilty one's back.

He can't help himself. The wild images are stronger than he is.

Given that I've never seen my father wearing pyjamas, nor swimming trunks, and certainly never without them, there is for me something astonishing and decidedly unseemly about looking into my great-grandfather's bedroom. But wasn't he the one who opened the door a crack and allowed me to look in?

Later the wild animal gets locked up in the conjugal cage. There it becomes tame. But his earlier wildness isn't forgotten, it's simply lying dormant within him.

In stages, he's drawn eastwards. From Cologne, where he completes a doctorate in law and obtains a first position in the legal system, to Halberstadt in Saxony. In 1890, at the age of twenty-six or twenty-seven, he gets himself transferred to the city known in German as Posen – or, to most of its population both now and at the time, Poznań.

I'd like to know how Poznań is pronounced, and find out that here too a large black window opens on the screen with a narrow grey strip in it and that again what I hear is not a robot's voice but a warm, masculine one. So were all my feelings 'merely' projections when I clicked on the word 'Oświęcim' and heard it spoken from that black window? Do the people who put these recordings into worldwide circulation treat each word the same way?

I listen to the two place names again several times, one after the other. The windows are indeed the same, large and black. But I stand firm: the voice that says 'Poznań', lively and vigorous, is that of a young man. 'Oświęcim' is pronounced by a man who is clearly older, in a low voice, almost toneless, cautious, restrained. The man who spoke that word had, consciously or involuntarily, also communicated what he knew.

Poznań: the accent is on the first syllable and the 'z' is a soft 's'. 'Pósnanyeh' is more or less how it sounds.

Why is the young official drawn to this eastern province of the German Empire, part of Prussia since 1815 but still Polish, where the German language is spoken only by a minority made up mostly of his fellow Protestants? He took up a post in the east of his own accord, I read. But what were his reasons? He certainly wasn't the kind of person to seek out the easiest path.

But why the east?

In a letter to the poet Richard Dehmel, his childhood friend Franz Servaes writes that Sanderling spent several years in the Poznań region as a 'germanisator *in partibus infidelium*', that is, as a person who went off to spread German culture in areas inhabited by unbelievers. In this case 'unbelievers' doesn't so much mean religious dissenters as those who aren't disciples of Deutschtum. It thus appears, or this at least is how his closest boyhood friend sees it, as if Sanderling went to Poznań in order actively to participate in the reinforcement of German culture that had been pursued by Bismarck and by the Prussian regimes that succeeded him.

From a book published in 1895, *Die geschlechtlich-sittlichen Verhältnisse der evangelischen Landbewohner im Deutschen Reiche* (The Sexual and Moral Conditions of

Protestant Country Dwellers in the German Empire), I learn how few Germans were living in the province of Poznań at this time, and also at what close quarters most people lived in the villages, often eight in two or three beds, and that the poverty was severe, filth everywhere and vermin widespread. Other sentences I note in this book include: 'It cannot readily be assumed that constant and close contact with the Polish Catholic population had an educational effect on hearts and minds and in morality, for it is hardly a secret that actual Poles are in this respect far from being moral role models.'

Actual Poles. Moral role models. Constant and close contact.

I read that in 1901, the Poles were described in the *Posener Tageblatt* as a 'backward and inferior people': 'In the Eastern March, the Germans are still the masters and not, as Polish presumptuousness would have us believe, guests – and we Germans wish to and shall remain the masters of this land!'

From various sources I also learn more than I'd like about 'Germanization measures' before and after the turn of the century, about the incremental banishment of the Polish language from public life and schools, first in secondaries and then in elementary schools. Finally even private language lessons in Polish are forbidden.

I'm relieved when it occurs to me that around the same time and until well into the twentieth century, the French Republic battled against its regional languages, for instance Breton. In schools in Brittany there were signs with the words IT IS FORBIDDEN TO SPEAK BRETON AND TO SPIT ON THE GROUND.

Does all this have anything in the least to do with Sanderling?

A thousand things go through my head at once, many of them contradictory and unclear, and I have the sense I ought to be able to convey how to read and feel and think about them at the same time, to create an image that the eye could take in all at once. Yet I have no choice but to follow the irreversible law of the book – for the reader as well as for the writer – according to which it must be one thing after the other. The book is the bearer of the inner image. The inner image can never show everything all at once, cannot confect simultaneity. But in that image, everything that is experienced and thought in the same instant can be focused as if in a single lens.

Ever since I set off on this journey into unfamiliar territory, heading towards my ancestor, I've had one image in my mind: I see a seemingly insurmountable mountain looming up between me and the man born a hundred years before me. An enormous massif, a giant mountain, made up of piles of dead bodies.

I don't even bother telling myself that he has nothing to do with those dead bodies, and that I've got nothing to do with them. So did they just fall from the sky or shoot up out of the earth between the two of us, between his existence and mine?

During a train journey heading east (for some even Stuttgart is the east), I talk to the person next to me, a

French writer, about my effort to get closer to my great-grandfather and about the impossibility of simply jumping over the time between us with hundred-year boots. As if what lay between us weren't a mountain but some gravel on the path.

He says: Fine, but we're all well aware of it, you know, what went on back in the 1940s.

We laugh.

But the giant mountain doesn't collapse. It's still there.

I say to my fellow passenger on the train: Well, maybe the mountain would disappear if I brought one of my great-grandfather's contemporaries back to life and commissioned them to write this book. But as long as *I'm* the author of this book, something towers between us, reaching way up above our heads. Call it what you will, I call it Poland.

He tells me he's slowly realizing what it must mean to be German. It's a burden you come into the world with, I say. It's been there from the start and never goes away. But you don't hold all the members of a family responsible for one person's crime! he says. That's dreadful. You can't let them do that to you, he says, you have to resist. He defends me, would like to acquit me, because in his eyes I've been wrongly accused. I tell him the question isn't whether you yourself feel guilty, whether such a feeling is justified or not. The burden is there, like it or not. Regardless of how violently you reject it. You feel it already even as a child. And, since from the start I've been feeling uncomfortable about seeming to appeal for his pity, I add: It's not so bad, it never keeps me from sleeping at night. That may be true, but only adds to it; I'd almost prefer it if from time to time it had prevented me from getting to sleep, I think, though I don't tell him this because it would strike him as unbelievable and exaggerated. I think.

Instead, I tell him that all German people, always and forever, will in their own and everyone else's eyes be associated with *that*. Germans experience this more clearly than ever when they're abroad. Quietly, I bark into his ear: *Achtung! Verboten!* And: *Ve haf vays off making you talk.*

My travelling companion: Right, that can't be very funny.

Me: Well, it is funny, but over time…

In any gathering of people of different nationalities – I don't just say this, I know it from long experience – a German person always stands for *that* and the others for nothing. No Russian represents the Gulag, no French person represents the French Revolution or colonialism. They do have their own national histories, but these lie behind them, as something they lean back on, as they would on a pillar. We carry ours like a sign (a scarlet letter) on our chests. The opposite of a shield. A target. No matter how we turn and twist, the sign always remains in front, perfectly visible.

My companion remembers that his grandparents always shuddered when they heard people near them speaking German. That generation has, however, all but disappeared now, he says.

Yet their grandchildren remember clearly how their grandparents shuddered when they heard people speaking German, I say.

Back at the Bibliothèque nationale, I open other books and read about the Deutsche Ostmarkenverein, a nationalist propaganda organization formed in Poznań, and about the 'Hakatists', named after the first letters of the names of the founders. Hakatists: it sounds like the clicking of military heels. I learn that the Poles living in Prussia, who in these eastern provinces accounted for about two thirds of the population, were in many respects disadvantaged in relation to the Germans. They were, however, better off than those of their compatriots who, in the most recent division of Poland, had been allocated to the Austrians or Russians.

Although many teachers and priests didn't speak Polish or spoke it poorly, they nevertheless were in no hurry to eradicate the language from the country since the vast majority of Poles spoke no German and were all the more resistant to learning it because their rulers wished to outlaw their native tongue. How can you teach, or preach, if you can't be understood?

Sanderling can't speak Polish either. Not a word, when he arrives in Posen/Poznań in 1890. Perhaps a few words, hello, thank you, how are you, when he returns to the West in 1904? He writes that to be understood by the few Polish Protestants, he asked a *young, fanatical* Polish vicar to teach him the language. But that young man soon ended the arrangement out of mistrust.

My great-grandfather doesn't settle in the countryside right away. For the first few years he lives in Poznań, the only city in the province, which around the turn of the century has about a hundred thousand inhabitants. Did the Germans, confident of their superiority, walk through the streets with their chests thrust forwards, like the colonial rulers they were?

In *Die Stadt Posen unter preußischer Herrschaft* (The City of Poznań under Prussian Rule) by Moritz Jaffé, published in 1909, I read that Germans and Poles 'do indeed pass by each other like strangers in the close quarters of present-day Poznań. Whether one frequents the city's high society or public amusements, or takes part in political meetings, or in artistic and scientific endeavours open to the public, one will find the two nationalities separated; not even sport or benevolent activities succeed in bringing them together. One hears the two languages mingling together in the city's streets, but it almost never happens that a German speaks Polish, and for a Pole to speak German only seldom.' Such a high degree of alienation between the two main segments of the population would, he says, have been unimaginable in the middle of the nineteenth century. What degree had that alienation reached by 1890?

Hoping to find out more, I get on with deciphering Sanderling's diaries from those years, scans of which I've now finally got on the screen in front of me. To begin with, I sit facing these handwritten pages as if they were covered in Chinese characters. I can't make out a single word or syllable. I'm forty-eight years old and must learn to read all over again. For days and weeks I peer at the jittery lines that nervously lean to the right, at the incomprehensible forward flight of the letters, their long loops cast like lassos. I stare at one word, then at another, and a third, without being any the wiser, and I'm seized with fury towards this great-grandfather, and the distance in time between us, which transforms everything. I throw in the towel. The next day, the staring starts all over again. And then? At some point? Yes, at some point, right there in the spot I've been staring at in vain for so long, a word appears. Slowly, very slowly, I make progress. I establish a new alphabet, Sanderling's alphabet; on a fresh piece of paper, I draw letters the way he forms them (not always the same) next to mine. I translate. In deciphering this alien handwriting, I feel as if I'm stepping from the open air into a darkened room and my eyes have to gradually get used to the new light conditions. New light conditions: does that capture what it's like, a different, faraway time?

I learn the 'e', I learn the 's'. With help of the letters I have deciphered, I learn how to guess the others. It's a riddle to be solved, a constellation to be made out in the sky of the past. I'm looking at a drawing and I know it represents something, but what? Until a word emerges from the thick fog of letters, then a second one, which unfortunately doesn't come right after the first but does allow me to gradually grope my way forwards.

Thanks to all this deciphering, the image of a journey through time turns into a process, an action. I can clearly sense the thick, tough mass that separates me from this relative who's older than me by a hundred years. To decipher his writing is to decipher a man. I'm feeling my way through the darkness towards my forefather. Trying to read him. To *understand* him. Before I travel to Poland, there are certain questions I'd like to ask him. Why did he move to this region, to Prussian Poland, and what was his life like there among Germans and Poles, Catholics, Jews and Protestants? When I finally succeed in catching the sense of what he writes, I'm surprised to find no answers to my questions. What did I imagine? Had I expected him to foresee how things would develop in Poland and Europe and thus what would one day torment his great-granddaughter?

The past can't provide any answers to today's questions. Our forebears had other things on their minds than wondering what we'd like to know from them. It appears that in Sanderling's Poznań/Posen, there are few Catholics and no Jews at all. For the most part, he lives there as he lived in Halberstadt, Saxony. His diaries aren't written for curious descendants. They contain observations about art, literature, religion and music. Aphorisms, maxims. Poems. Lots of prayers. His diary entries are answers to questions I don't ask myself. Where am I going to find answers to my questions? In Poland?

I do, however, learn from his diaries about his love affair with a Polish woman he got to know during the very first year of his time in Poznań. Her name is the first word in his notes that is clearly legible – whether that's because he wants to highlight the name of his lover, or because the Polish doesn't flow easily from his pen. Pelagia Kruszczyńska. He calls her 'Pela'. What does she call him? She's very unhappy and goes on tenderly loving him when he leaves her. He can recall, he writes, having shed tears twice as an adult: in front of his mother on one occasion, and when he said goodbye to Pela. Why does he leave her only a few months after they met? That's not revealed by the diary; at most, one can guess from a few passages. Sanderling wants to get married, wishes to escape his previous lifestyle, which he experiences as sinful and agonizing. But Pela isn't a suitable bride for him. He doesn't say why not, so I'm left with conjecture, and unfortunately my first thought is: because she's Polish? Because she's poor and Catholic and uneducated? He doesn't write anything like that, or at least I can't decipher anything along those lines. Instead he admits that his love faded away like an episode of drunkenness, leaving him with nothing to crave – everything he desired, he has already had. Perhaps that and that alone is the reason for the break-up, and any other interpretations tell us less about this man lost in the past than they do about me.

He leaves her, and afterwards loves her almost more even than before. He loves and respects her, because the woman he left continues to feel tenderness and love towards him. And as late as two years later, on the day he gets married, the memory of that love will haunt him. A guilty conscience will cast a shadow over his wedding.

Sanderling's son, my grandfather, narrated this episode in his biographical sketch of his father. What did he make it into? *A love idyll with the beautiful, hot-blooded but dirt-poor Polish girl Pelagia. To leave her, he had to go through hard and bitter struggles; and yet all he did was free himself from the intolerable fetters of a sensual passion.*

Love idyll. Beautiful, hot-blooded, but dirt poor. Intolerable fetters of sensual passion. Why do you need your own language, or even your own experiences, if you can attach to the words 'Polish girl' the most obvious adjectives and simply stamp an expiry date on a love that doesn't befit the person's rank?

Not long after this, Sanderling falls for a young German woman named Agnes, but she already *holds another in her heart*. Then, in November 1892: Emma, soon called Emmachen (little Emma), and it's a short distance from there to a wedding, and then Emmachen becomes Mieze.

I'm living beyond my means and I have debts, he writes during the period of his engagement. Within a few years he goes from man about town to married man and finally man of the cloth. With great difficulty, I decipher this passage from 1895: *One day recently, something remarkable happened to me. I came through from my desk, where I had been working on some insignificant tasks, and sat down at the dinner table when Mieze, without pausing at all as she did so, uttered the name Luise* (instead of 'the name Luise', Sanderling's deceased sister, I initially read 'the name Luther', and think the man has succumbed entirely to a Protestant delirium). *I at once became as if spellbound. I felt as if all the dining room were filling up with Luise's spirit, as if she were intrinsically there and yet not physically present and was looking down on our familial contentment with gentle sympathy.* Once again the time separating us tries to make an interpretation and goad me into sneering at my forefather and his visions. The spirit of the dead sister *looks down on* the familial contentment! The time separating us is trying to make a spirit out of me too, but one that instead of looking down on this idyll with gentle sympathy does so with outright derision. I resist that interference. Leave me alone, time. What I feel is more like longing for a world in which the impalpable still manifested itself.

When I came back and my wife asked me if I'd been feeling unwell, I briefly told her about the visitation, but in spite of my assuring her it was friendly and not in the least frightening, she convulsively fell into emitting appalling screams and, out of terror at the supposedly ghastly phenomenon, became seized, physically and mentally, with terrible shudders.

Sanderling talks about Emma/Mieze as if she is a highly sensitive, tender, submissive child. Transplanting such a person to the most remote Polish villages, expecting her to deal with continual changes of location and profession – Sanderling will later become a priest – is certainly not what a psychiatrist, had one been consulted, would have recommended. And indeed, only a few years after their marriage, Emma spends some time in a psychiatric hospital. The doctors recommend that Sanderling get himself transferred from his first pastorate in Wilczkowice (German: Wolfskirch) where he presides over a large Protestant community, to a quieter place. Thus the family arrives in Połajewo.

In the previously mentioned book by Moritz Jaffé, I stumble across the name of a man whom I'm aware Sanderling not only knew well, but admired and even loved. He counted him among the rare *people who function like a filter, cleansing the murky water that flows through him from other people and returning it to them purified. Pure filters who possess such depths, such a bottomless pit of forgiveness and forgetting, such a living, clarifying stream of compassion, that all the human misery and filth doesn't remain in their consciousness, doesn't muddy and contaminate their own being but rather sinks down into mysterious depths that are protected and hidden by God Himself.*

This man, Johannes Hesekiel, whom Sanderling in another passage calls a saint, was the 'General Superintendent' of Poznań province, thus a kind of deacon, and he worked for the Inner Mission, a movement that operated (and still does) within the Protestant Church. And so I read about the Inner Mission, whose founder Johann Hinrich Wichern selected Hesekiel to collaborate with him and who among other things founded the 'Rauhe Haus' in Hamburg, through which he aimed to provide a home for orphans and other abandoned children, who were roaming the streets and stealing. Such were the circles Sanderling became part of in Poland, people who dedicated themselves to *love that saves* and wished to take care equally of the souls and bodies of the poorest and most helpless.

And because I'm not carrying out research for a historical study but groping forwards, following intuitions and associations and thus sometimes getting stuck on a single word or name, I open up the Old Testament and read the Book of Ezekiel.

I read: 'The hand of the Lord was upon me, and carried me out in the spirit of the Lord, and set me down in the midst of the valley which was full of bones.'

I read: 'Then he said unto me, Son of man, these bones are the whole house of Israel: behold, they say, Our bones are dried, and our hope is lost: we are cut off for our parts.'

I read: 'Behold, I will cause breath to enter into you, and ye shall live. And I will lay sinews upon you, and will bring up flesh upon you, and cover you with skin, and put breath in you, and ye shall live; and ye shall know that I am the Lord.'

I read: 'And they lived, and stood up upon their feet, an exceeding great army.'

Is that the army that's been escorting me all along as I've moved back and forth in time, wrapped in a maelstrom of fine threads through which everything seems to be connected, without any of them being the direct cause of any other?

I'm trying to gain access to a small world, that of the Protestant community of Poznań before the turn of the century, and to the even smaller one of those devoted to charitable work, led and embodied by one good person – why should I doubt his goodness? – called Johannes Hesekiel. Under his influence, a young official in the Prussian government, who is not yet anywhere near being my great-grandfather, conceives the wish to leave administration to others and henceforth to serve not the state, but God and His creatures. He's over thirty and already has a wife and a child when he makes the decision to study theology and become a priest. The first real decision in his life is one that causes him to drop out of all the usual career paths and ambitions. There aren't many people who, having made it onto the straight track of officialdom with its regular stations, each higher than the last, break ranks in order to devote all their strength to their fellow human beings – and to the being furthest away from them.

Kindness, gentleness, solicitude. Forgiveness. Compassion. Those seem to be the qualities Sanderling felt emanated from Hesekiel and which attracted him and drew him to the Church and into the Church. Some consider Hesekiel stupid. People are always ready to call kindness and gentleness stupidity. Yet *Saints cannot be judged by the measure of cleverness.*

Severity, rigidity, implacability. Fervour. Obstinacy. *Iron rhythm and tone.* That's what he ends up encountering in Greifswald, where he takes up the study of theology. The man who in himself unites those qualities is theology professor Hermann Cremer.

For someone to be equally attracted to and influenced by two such antagonistic characters, they must, it seems to me, carry in themselves some of those peculiarities, at least in embryo or else as a longed-for, sought-after goal. Or simply as the old, protean pair that has always sparred within us: hard and soft, loud and quiet, warm and cold.

I look at a picture of Cremer, the fleshy nose, the disdainfully downward-pointing corners of the mouth, and alongside it Hesekiel's Father Christmas face, his bald head with full beard. It looks as if someone grabbed him by the hair and pulled it down on the other side of his head all the way to the chin. It's easier for Hesekiel, the warm and benevolent one, to last in the long term. Time is against Cremer. To appreciate Cremer's idiosyncrasies as they perhaps deserve, I would have to forget the century that stretches out between us, and ideally also myself.

There's his rejection of any doubt. His certainty in all matters of faith. It is not permitted to raise any questions, to express the least uncertainty. Not at any time! In Sanderling's notes I read: *In Greifswald there was no hope of any future development of Christianity to a higher level, because absolute certainty prevailed. In Greifswald no historical critique could gain a foothold; you took note of it and remained certain. You were hostile towards any kind of religious exaltation; you didn't feel, you were certain.* So much certainty in one man is either stupidity or – more likely – the sign of a deep perplexity concealed at all costs.

That certainty is accompanied by a rigour and harshness scarcely imaginable a hundred years later: *My wife and I soon became friends with these two passionate Christians. In one conversation, someone asked what stance a Christian should take towards the prevailing custom in prosperous circles of making use of wet nurses in child-rearing. We had taken on a wet nurse for our eldest child, but our consciences were troubled about it. For the wet nurses, who often came from the Spree forest region, were fallen women who in a sense exploited and sold their extramarital motherhood. Wasn't a Christian facilitating the path of fornication by hiring these illegitimate mothers and women for their own child-rearing? I didn't do it when I found myself in that situation, said the wife of the theology professor Cremer. But if the child didn't thrive when fed from the bottle? I asked. It would still be wrong, she said, to encourage others to commit sin merely to make things easier for your own flesh and blood. But what if it's a matter of life and death for the child? Even then, she replied. And what happened with your child? I asked her. Almost without any trembling in her voice, the answer came: I let my child die for the Lord.*

Time intervenes between us, a wall with no windows. It prevents any *putting yourself in their place*. I can register it: ah, back then people thought and felt differently. Christians would rather let their children die than have them nourished with disreputable milk. But how am I supposed to regard these individuals from the past as anything other than deluded and deranged? It also doesn't help much to realize that if they got a look at me from the afterlife, they wouldn't feel any different. I've *familiarized myself* with the period, grappled with pietism, Protestant dogma, with various conditions of the time that could serve as explanations, to no avail. I genuinely can *comprehend*, within certain limits. But I cannot, at least at this point, *empathize*. And isn't it precisely empathy that needs to succeed if a bridge is to be built, if we are to hear what these people from the past had that's present-day, even eternal?

Sanderling reproduces this conversation without any sign of disapproval; on the contrary, he appears impressed by the rigour and implacability these *passionate Christians* display even towards themselves. He doesn't write whether or not he imitated Cremer's ruthlessness and dismissed the wet nurse who was in his employ. The thought makes me shudder. And there we are again, face to face, as if both alive: Sanderling is small and gaunt, still quite young – he never did grow very old – and I look into the bright glow in his eyes. He stands up straight yet I'm a head taller than him; I stand to my full height before him and I have his nose and his mouth and his forehead. A plane slowly passes by the window, we don't look at it, we look at each other. And then? And then the corners of his mouth rise barely perceptibly, and he smiles at me with my lips. And I don't carry on with him the conversation I'd like to, I don't ask what would have happened if Pela or the one-armed girl had got pregnant, I don't ask him about his years of *fornication*, which he calls his *man-about-town period*, before his marriage, I don't tell him how my mother bound her belly for seven months while I lay in there all curled up yet nonetheless getting steadily bigger, how finally she could no longer hide her belly nor its contents from her own parents, in whose house she was living, how her father, my grandfather, never spoke to her again, how I was also a thorn in the side of my other grandfather, *his* son, who for his whole life would have nothing to do with me. I don't tell him all that because I know, I can tell by looking at him, that he would not have let his child die, and that's enough for me. Right now it's enough for me. I look at him, am on the point of taking a step towards him, when he dissolves before my eyes. I can still see his quiet smile, then he's vanished.

Prosperous circles. As a priest-to-be, he doesn't necessarily belong in such circles, but he did marry a woman from a well-to-do family. Women in these circles don't breastfeed their own children. Breastfeeding is a base, bestial activity – albeit less bestial, it appears, than actually giving birth to children, which you apparently have to undertake yourself, for better or worse – for which you engage the services of a maid. The counterpart to the playboy is the fallen woman. No fallen women, no playboys. Any kind of support provided to these fallen women would amount to retroactive absolution or forgiveness; therefore, anything that might ease their lives must be avoided. If you are a stickler about it, at least. And the Cremers are sticklers. Passionate sticklers. The disciplining of women unknown to you who have sinned is more important than the life of your own child. The child is sacrificed to God, you let it die *for the Lord*.

This rigour he encounters, but which he also feels in himself, has a beguiling effect on Sanderling. (All these affirmative statements could be incorrect; that goes without saying and will therefore only be mentioned here once.) It beguiles him all the more because everything in him is fracturing and breaking apart. He needs that rigour, he nurtures it, solidifies it, to the point where a caress is more painful for him than a physical blow. That's later on. He's been a priest for some years. The post he wanted with all his soul and for which he once again started again from the beginning – or not so much the post itself as its incompatibility with earthly reality – bears down on him not like sacks of grain or tons of concrete but with the weight of God Himself. The people in the Polish villages aren't especially concerned about their souls and also don't ask anyone else to preoccupy themselves with them. There are other things they need more. Could Jesus be the doctor who will heal people and livestock, that's the kind of question they ask. They need material help, they need bread.

An old man, Johannes Hesekiel, the good person of Posen, senses Sanderling's distress. But he does not want at any price to be considered a person in need; what Hesekiel grants him in this moment, *the best thing* he received during these years, is at the same time experienced by him as *the worst thing*: a caress. *An expression of helplessness, of woe and weariness, must have appeared on my face, whose mask I otherwise so resolutely master. For old Father Hesekiel, who had stood up and walked past my seat, stroked my cheek as if to comfort me. For years I hadn't been able to remember this without feeling a hot stain of shame.*

To be a weak person in need of being comforted, or worse still, to be perceived as such by another, is more humiliating than being punched in the face. He would like to be made of steel, inside and out. He'd like to be that way, I imagine, because he's so far from being that way. He may have dedicated himself to *Love that saves*, which is what the Inner Mission promises people. But under no circumstances does he wish to be someone who needs saving, to be a person who suffers inner distress. *He* is the one who helps others stand up, who pulls them up to his level, not the other way around. There's a pride here, an extreme rigour towards himself, that it's hard for me to see as compatible with benevolence and gentleness towards others.

In order to find out more about Sanderling's life, I bury myself in his autobiographical notes, which along with a wealth of other writings in his hand are now preserved in the Walter Benjamin Archive in Berlin. While Benjamin did not become his executor – a role for which Sanderling designated him – their estates did end up in the same place: the archive in question. So one afternoon I'm sitting in a building in Berlin-Mitte, Luisenstraße 60, in which Karl Marx is supposed to have lived between October 1838 and March 1839, and which looks the way I imagine an East German government office to. I pore over Sanderling's papers next to researchers who possibly feel closer to the subject of their research than I do to mine, even though (or perhaps because) they aren't related to theirs. The estate consists of lots of book drafts, manuscripts, diaries and letters, all meticulously organized and stored in clean binders and stacked up on labelled shelves. The door that allows access to the windowless archive room, while not exactly armoured, is made of heavy metal. Humidity and temperature are regulated, I assume. For reasons I'm not sure about and which in any case have no significance for anyone besides me, I only want to read these papers now they're locked up in here, although until a few years ago they lay around at my father's place in boxes or trunks.

Two or three of the dossiers are lying in front of me in the reading room, and I pull the paper folders out one at a time, as carefully as if I were holding one of the earliest Bibles, a papyrus scroll that had been buried for centuries and only just brought to light. Weren't those sacred texts hidden many centuries ago specifically so they wouldn't fall into the hands of non-believers or others unworthy of them? Which here might mean philistines, amateurs, non-specialists. I see the Walter Benjamin Archive as the shrine of one of the most valuable intellectual treasures hidden in the innermost rooms of the temple, and myself as a poorly disguised spy who's somehow managed to gain entry.

First I want to see if any light from the past can shine far enough to reach me, whether somewhere a corner will peek out, the end of a thread I can pull on.

It's very quiet in the reading room. Apart from me there are only two young researchers, sitting some distance away from me. When we lift up our heads from our scrolls, we look at the windows and beyond them the dull grey facade of the office building on the other side of the street. Each of us sits here in this sober room with other living beings and also in the company of the dead. In another, distant time. We can't be in that distant time in the same way as those who lived then were; we're like travellers who go to spend time among Inuit people or Pygmies, in any case in an unfamiliar land, about which they learned a certain amount beforehand yet which ultimately remains closed to them. We've read the country's literature, acquainted ourselves with the indigenous people's habits of thought and perception, yet we still only see two-dimensional images, strange-looking hairstyles, items of clothing, gestures. We're unable to reach the people. But I tell myself that if I live among them for a longer time, as ethnologists did, perhaps I'll manage to reduce the distance by a few millimetres.

There are physical changes we can't overcome, my French travelling companion told me on our train journey east. Human beings in earlier times weren't constituted the same; their brains were different.

Certainly an insurmountable obstacle remains, a mountain or a gulf. But isn't there a difference between the person who stands on the edge of the gulf shrugging and the one who exerts themselves to the full and employs all possible strategies to cross it? If the inner exertion, like the outer exertion, functions as a mode of transport, the second person does in the end get somewhat closer. But what are we to make of the many people who don't even notice that there is an obstacle? Who in describing earlier times don't even make the effort to transport themselves back in time, but on the contrary, as if it were possible, transplant those who are no more into the present? As if time is a conveyor belt whose sole purpose is to deposit everything that ever existed at their feet while they sit back comfortably in their armchairs.

I'm sitting in the archive, bent over some of the papers Sanderling left behind. Having put on the white cotton gloves I've been given for this purpose, I first reach for his shabby address book. Before I take the miniature spatula, about the length of a fork, that's another item in my archive equipment, and delicately slide it between the pages, I study what remains of the sharkskin or galuchat binding, with its dark, dull pearl pattern; the pale-red letter tabs down the right side are thin and bent with age, and some of them are missing, beginning with A and C: the teeth that fell out of the alphabet. The B tab is barely still attached. And how strange it feels to find, between the names *von Bötticher* (Carl Wilhelm, a senior Prussian official) and *Brouwer* (a Dutch professor of mathematics), the name *Benjamin, W*, with the address *Grunewald, Delbrückstr.* 23; above it, in parentheses, something illegible ending in the digits 1488, possibly a telephone number. Elsewhere, similarly squeezed in among unfamiliar names, *v. Hofmannsthal, Hugo, Rodaun bei Wien*. These names are scattered as unthinkingly and indiscriminately as all the Smiths, Webers and Joneses in our address books, the famous and the forgotten, friend and foe right next to each other under the shared roof of one letter. Through careful handling of the spatula, I see a web that extends, in the early 1920s, from Berlin to Vienna (*Mayröcker, Frau Dr Hofrat*), from Munich (*Scholem, Gershom, Munich, Türckstraße 98*) via Holland (*van Eeden*) to New York (*Oppenheimer, Franz, Maiden Lane, NY*). As if in a group photograph taken shortly before a shipwreck, they're all gathered together one last time in the address book. Before removing the cotton gloves and turning to Sanderling's autobiographical fragments, I slide the unspoiled world of the address book back into its binder. *Heile Welt*, the world of before, the unspoiled world: one of those concepts, like Sehnsucht or Heimat, that only exist and therefore can only be expressed in German.

Some parts of the autobiographical sketch are typed and therefore easy to read. In those sections, Sanderling writes about his life as a pastor in the Poznań region, about his daily tasks *which covered my soul in detritus* and which consisted, for example, of disputes over school finances, alleged cases of perjury, and having coffee with the schoolmaster's wife. *Detritus* seems to mean more or less the same thing as *the everyday*, if by that you understand trifling matters, small deceptions (including of yourself), pettiness that swallows people whole. Had he been an idealist of the same kind as his parents, believing in attainable, quotidian ideals, then perhaps he would have blossomed in his priest's role, or at least have found it satisfying. He would, to the best of his ability, have accomplished what could be accomplished, and helped others to do the same. The unattainable would not have weighed with unimaginable and absolute force on his shoulders, nor on those of his young son. For as he writes later, he took his son out of school because the teacher inspired no confidence in him. This was, he says, a terrible time for father and child. *My patience snapped more often than was right. But the bad thing was that every time it snapped, and with every reprimand, and in general in the whole atmosphere of the lesson, the oppressive power of an authority bore down on the child, an authority which carried far more weight than that of a normal teacher and wasn't merely the authority of a father, a very serious father, but that of a priest who carried the burdens of all of humanity and divinity and himself felt unhappy carrying them.*

He rebels against the God who encumbered him with that burden without giving him shoulders that could have carried it. He rails against the people around him, their mindlessness, the unspiritual lives they lead. He suffers from his own *so frightfully grave nature* which makes him suited neither to teaching (though as a clergyman he's supposed to do that) nor to being a village pastor. He's *bird*, he's *phoenix*, he's *man of the hereafter*: does it make any sense *to expect this temporal realm to resemble that realm*? For he finds himself surrounded by a world that is entirely profane. The vague hereafter that sometimes shines forth for him, that he craves and divines but which repeatedly evades him, he finds no trace of in the eyes of the others, in their gestures, in the soulless treadmill of their daily tasks. Least of all in those who, by virtue of office, status and religion, are closest to him: the *normal Prussian Christians*, his German *brothers in faith* who have nothing brotherly about them. He's a stranger among them. There's no one he could make feel or at least understand his anguish, even if he could capture it in words. No one in whom a similar rift might have opened up. Towards the end of his time in the east, he is alone, though his solitude strikes nobody besides him. From morning to night he wears his iron mask. No one supports him because no one sees his distress. The only person who suspects anything, benevolent old Hesekiel, has nothing more than compassion to offer him. And he, without realizing it, pushes him further still into solitude and despair. Since no help can be expected from the living, Sanderling seeks support among the dead, whose *living voices* talk to him. *I conferred with Goethe*. Not something every soul in need can say of themselves. But why shouldn't someone who talks to God and wishes to call Him to account not also confer with Goethe? He also talks with Nietzsche, but in that case it feels to him like a soliloquy. Neither the dead nor the living can alleviate his distress. He is at a loss. *I was like a pause in my own being.*

During this period a conference takes place with other pastors; today we'd probably call it something like 'continuing pastoral education'. Sanderling shares a room with one of these men, can't tear the mask away from his face even for a second. On the first day, he's appointed to say matins. He feels it keenly: *a prayer such as I needed to pray was one the others could never have prayed with me.* Yet he has no choice; the usual litany isn't within his range. Or perhaps it is, yes, maybe he does reach for it, reaches for anything he might take hold of, even empty husks of prayers in use every day, and fills them up with his profound forsakenness, thrusts them out with the full force of his affliction. There's something in his voice that separates him from the others. They don't so much pray with him as furtively observe their *brother minister*. For to them, there's something unseemly, embarrassing about the fervour erupting out of him.

He prays too desperately, and above all he prays for too long. Gently – old Hesekiel is the one who takes on the task – he's interrupted and asked to conclude. Ten minutes were planned, and he's already been talking for more than quarter of an hour. Breakfast awaits. And the day's programme. That consists of some *instructive excursions*; more precisely, of visits to a prison and an asylum.

The first institution they visited that morning was, according to Sanderling's notes, both district workhouse and penitentiary. Were poor people punished for their poverty? It seems more likely that they were two separate establishments under the same roof. *It was abundantly clear that the director, an erstwhile major, was afraid these pastors he was obliged to show around might wish not just to save the prisoners' souls but to rescue them from the institution. We were enjoined not to exchange a single word with them. Like a gang of prisoners, we were led past the other prisoners.*

I'm right there with him, reading, and I feel pleasure at having a great-grandfather like this. One who lives in the most extreme inner isolation, who doesn't wangle his way through any situation but who holds himself to the highest standards; one who is more sensitive and who feels more deeply than other people do. Then comes the visit to the *lunatic asylum*.

What I now read hits me like a slap in the face (and not the way one of Hesekiel's caresses struck Sanderling). I'm going to reproduce the passage in its entirety, even though I can't rid myself of the feeling that I'm doing its author an injustice. Every quotation, every excerpt from a whole is unjust; how much more so in a case like this. Yet it shall be included here, along with many others. I do wish, however, for it to be read in the same way as all the previous ones – as a small sample that can't do justice to the person speaking.

We were led through the same institution where the former pastor of the neighbouring parish had for decades turned out insipid sermons and where I'd brought Ortlieb and Frau Niewöhner. There they were still, the idiotic children, being fed like animals or gluing cardboard boxes together and soiling themselves, and healthy people gave their labour in exchange for money to sustain those incapable of work and in a higher sense incapable of living, creatures whose relatives could no longer tolerate having them close by and whom all of us were too cowardly to eradicate from the face of the earth; too cowardly. I saw the huge red walls of this establishment's vast buildings, I saw the army of officials, the stream of gold that was necessary to sustain all of this and these few mentally ill people, I saw the mindlessness in my Połajewo parish and the poverty and the unfocused longings of those who really had vitality, and I wondered, why don't you direct your gold, your services, your working life towards the enhancement of lives that can be enhanced, instead of to the preservation of lives that can't achieve anything, and I looked at all us blackcoats, and I said to myself, it's because we clerics are afraid, and we're terrifying in our fear, the way we whimper for our poor lives, even if we disguise it as eternal life, because for us there's nothing greater than to live quand même, *that's why we tie the hands of everyone and prevent anyone from taking another's life. That's why you preach the way you do, Hesekiel, that's why you doctors toe the line, and I asked the assistant doctor I'd joined: why don't you poison these people? The man smiled ironically. His smile meant: why do Christians forbid it? But how marvellous: one of the patients said it himself, a splendid man, a Rubenesque Hercules. He stood naked by the wall of his room or his cell. 'Kill me,' he yelled at the doctor when we entered. There followed a stream of insults and a stream of accusations, which conveyed that he was suffering atrociously. 'Kill me,' he shouted, 'but you don't have the courage!' We were pulled back, and the door quickly closed. The fine young doctor next to me was still smiling ironically. In my heart, I applauded him for that, since I thought more highly of him than of us priests. But the most inwardly impressive human being I saw that day was the insane Hercules, and I applauded him in my heart as I swore to myself: I don't wish to be smaller than you, I don't wish to be as small as the Christian God.*

It begins with my username, which is 'Panzerdivision'. That was the first sentence of this book. Now, after a few dozen pages, it seems to me that there's another starting point, further and deeper back in time. How does it really begin?

I'm no longer sitting in Berlin but at a window in Normandy. Around me, all is quiet and peaceful. Outside it's calmer than it almost ever is in this village not far from the sea, where the summer stretches out in front of me like a big white page. I think of a passage in a book by Otto Dov Kulka, look for the book, find the page: 'The colour is blue: clear blue skies of summer. Silver-coloured toy aeroplanes carrying greetings from distant worlds pass slowly across the azure skies, while around them explode what look like white bubbles. The aeroplanes pass by and the sky remains blue and lovely, and far off, far off on that clear summer day, distant blue hills as though not of this world make their presence felt. That was the Auschwitz of that eleven-year-old boy.'

The quiet of early summer consists of the sound of the past. The longer I sit and listen, the better I can hear that sound; behind the high bird calls I hear the dark voices, no less incomprehensible, of the dead.

It begins with the shadow you can't get rid of. You'd have to be able to sell it, like Schlemihl in that story by Chamisso. But it's not easy to find a taker for the shadow I'm talking about. Not even the Devil wants it.

I never knew my father's father, even though he didn't die until I was already an adolescent. I was one of those things that happened but that people paid no attention to: an illegitimate child. That he was a *dear Grandpa* is something I found out from my legitimate siblings.

It begins with the memory. With the fact that in old age, childhood and youth come to life again while the many decades in between fade out. A known phenomenon. Thus my father talks more and more often about the past. He was seventeen when the war came to an end. Shortly before, like thousands of others, he had been mobilized as an anti-aircraft auxiliary. The Americans who took him prisoner placed him on the hood of their jeep and jolted back to their unit with this easily captured figurehead. He had been sent out by his fellow soldiers, those with only walk-on parts, to scavenge a loaf of bread in the next village, and so, when the Americans aimed their guns at him, he still had a loaf under his arm. So, I asked him, did he put his hands in the air as he was ordered to? No, he said, he couldn't, because of the loaf of bread. They took that from him, along with the hand grenades he had in his jacket pockets. Then they took him to a prison camp in Normandy, not far from the village I'm sitting in right now and where today the weather is unusually calm.

Another phenomenon that's equally well known and is generally excoriated is the silence that reigned in Germany after the war. In a study of the Nazi era, and of how it lives on in families' memories, I read that this silence was more or less invented by the 1968 generation; they carefully cultivated the myth of a silent war generation because they themselves didn't want to talk. This seems doubtful to me, but ultimately I can't be the judge, since I interact only with people and not with generations.

In the American prison camp where my father lived along with many other German teenagers, none of whom had ever known anything other than the Nazi regime, he tells me there was plenty of keeping silent. They did talk, of course. But the thousand-year Reich of their childhood and youth that had just come to an end (both the Reich and their youth), and in which their parents and most of them had at least to some extent firmly believed, that was something on which they didn't waste any words.

I try to imagine it: hundreds of lanky adolescent boys, locked in a confined space for months on end – to them forever – their thoughts behind the barbed wire constantly revolving around a blind spot. But I think that's the wrong way to conceive of it. They lived there together, waiting to be allowed to go home. They knew nothing about any blind spot. It took fifty or sixty years for that blind spot to spread itself out inside their heads. Like one of those small stains you try to get out with soap and water only to discover, once the fabric has dried, that a much larger stain, an aureole, has appeared. A shadow.

When my father was allowed to go back home, his father hadn't yet returned. He too was in a camp: in the British internment camp in Hemer, Westphalia, which until recently had been the so-called Stalag VI A. In that camp, tens of thousands of mostly Russian prisoners of war had been forced to labour in the mines in the Ruhr and elsewhere, and many of them died. You can consider such things as facts, and acknowledge them, just as you have acknowledged the existence of other camps, without ultimately being able to make sense of it all. Transit camps, internment camps, prison camps, penal camps, re-education camps, concentration and extermination camps: there were dozens, hundreds, perhaps thousands of them. As if at that time there was no other place for the people of Europe to stay.

After the end of the war, Stalag VI A was converted into a penal and re-education camp for presumed National Socialists. When my grandfather returned home from there, in the spring or perhaps summer of 1946, he had, according to my father, become a devout Christian. Even though this family thought well of itself, they behaved as many others did: in the following decades, there was never any talk either of the barking man with the little moustache, or of anything that had happened during his reign. My siblings and I have extended that silence into the present. Not that I'd have dared ask. Perhaps I shied away from doing so, but that wasn't the real reason. Above all, out of childish spite, I wanted nothing to do with these grandparents who hadn't even been willing to set eyes on the little girl I was. Though they never learned anything about this laughable, belated punishment, I punished them by paying as little attention to them as they had to me. I was forty when I first saw photos of these people. By that point they were long dead. Many more years then went by, during which my individual, defiant disinterest, my refusal to ask questions, coincided with the general silence, sometimes called leaden, of the German people.

Only in the last few years, well over half a century after the end of the war, does my father talk when I visit him about the silence that weighs more and more heavily on his conscience. He no longer understands it, he tells me; he reproaches himself for it.

I travel from Normandy to where he lives in the Rhineland. During the two days I spend there, our conversation frequently turns to the past. Was your father an opportunistic or a committed Nazi? I ask him. One who wanted to build his career or at least retain his position, or one who genuinely believed in the 'cause'? I ask this as if no third possibility exists. But presumably there is not only a third but a thousand other possible ways to have been a Nazi. Besides which, in asking the question, I'm not clear which of the two would have been more desirable. Perhaps, though, I'd have preferred a stupid, sincere person to a lucid one with no scruples.

My father was a committed Nazi, he replies.

Despite my preference for credulous blockheads, this doesn't elicit cheers from me.

I ask him if he understands how a man whose father, Sanderling, for whom he felt great admiration, who had many Jewish friends – and not just alibi Jews but genuine, close friends: Benjamin, Buber, Scholem, Rosenzweig, Gutkind – and who moreover felt the deep bond that connected him, as a Christian, to Judaism, how the son of such a man could have become an 'ardent' Nazi.

He can't understand it. That rupture, that ominous shadow, weighs on his chest. He tells me he knew his parents' Jewish friends very well when he was a young man, and that after the war he tried to reconnect with some of those who had survived the twelve-year Reich by emigrating. Understandably, most of them curtly turned him down, and no further exchange came about. When my father travelled to America for the first time in the early 1950s, he went to see Erich and Lucie Gutkind. He shows me their reply to a letter from his father, in which they protested against having been named as guarantors in a visa application to enter America, without having been asked beforehand. Yet their letter ends with these words: 'And if your son wishes to bring us a spark of the old fire, that will give us great pleasure.' Once he was there, he tells me, the two of them did indeed welcome him warmly, two nice old people sitting opposite him in their tiny New York apartment. And here too everyone kept silent. Over half a century later, my father feels ashamed that he sat in this couple's home and presumably accepted their hospitality while offering no explanation and saying nothing about the fundamental issue, and I love and honour him for that shame. I tell myself it's the most precious thing we have. The burning of that shame lasts decades, gets passed on; not held up high like an Olympic flame but quietly entrusted to the next person. I'm grateful to my father for that.

Perhaps the Gutkinds don't know that one of their old friend's sons was a Nazi. They are friendly to my father. They don't ask any questions, not even of this young man they're entertaining in their home. Some things must have been reported to them. Or maybe not. They suspect plenty. And yet they are friendly. Because they're incapable of hatred and harshness? Because those few people in Germany, the descendants of their friends, are the only connection to the life they once had, their intellectual world and their language.

Erich Gutkind's mother, Elise Gutkind, born in Weinberg in 1942, died in Theresienstadt. That's something I'll find out later, back in Normandy, on the internet.

The Gutkinds, my father says, and in my mind that name Gutkind, which means good child, gets mixed up in a strange way with my image of this old couple of emigrants, friendly *despite everything*, and the title of Erich Gutkind's major work, which appears to be a mystical study: *Siderische Geburt* (Sideric Birth). I don't remember, if I ever did know, what 'sideric' means, but I do know the French word sidérant. It refers to extreme bafflement, a kind of numbness or stupor.

The Gutkinds. I remember a passage in a book I recently read by Karl Emil Franzos. It describes how in the eighteenth century the Jews of Hungary, Galicia and Bukovina had last names forced upon them. This took place in the reign of Joseph II, the same emperor who established a fortified town in Bohemia and in honour of his mother called it Theresienstadt. These names were often made up of German words combined, as is the case with Gutkind. The arbitrary imposition of names by imperial royal officers was intolerable to the Jews, since they bore Hebrew names that were sacred to them. Furthermore, there was corruption: those who didn't want to have an insulting name, who didn't want to be called Galgenholz (gallows wood), Blutsauger (bloodsucker), Thränenvergießer (tear weeper) or Falscherhund (cheating dog) often had to pay a bribe. One passage of Franzos's book that stayed with me concerns an older man who lived with his wife and daughter in a cottage by the river. He gives no reply to the question of what he wishes to be called. He cries and moans. So he is named Weinstein. And the next one Steinwein. And so on. I imagine that when the officers tasked with assigning names found themselves face to face with the Gutkinds' grandparents, they didn't have to think about it for long.

My father told me how he's also still tormented by the idea that in 1944 his parents moved into an apartment in Bielefeld that was directly above the offices of the secret service for the SS. In Grünstraße. An apartment like that would only have been assigned to someone the regime could trust, and only a faithful Party member would have accepted it. Receiving visits from dissidents in this building was inconceivable. But what dissidents could have visited anyway? The Jewish friends had emigrated a long time ago; Benjamin had already taken his own life.

I look at my father, sitting there, sunk into himself, in his Eames Lounge Chair designed in 1956, one specimen of which is in the Museum of Modern Art in New York, another in my father's living room. I see a man who's now old, indeed in his dotage, with all the humiliating frailty he tries to hide and which, it seems to me, has brought him closer to me. And two feelings are alive in me at once, the first being my distress over the fact that he is permanently right on the edge of the abyss, that for some time now his existence has seemed to be hanging by a thread. When he gets up and walks a few steps, it seems as if he might collapse any minute, and I'm on the alert, ready to jump up and catch him. He refuses to use a cane. As for the device on wheels that you push in front of yourself, he hasn't so much as uttered its name. And at the same time there's also something else.

The awful thought occurs to me that of all the things from the past that weigh upon him, what might well hurt the most is the banal and vulgar fact of having had a Nazi for a father. And that this might also be at the root of his silence. By talking to me and perhaps to others close to him, he's opened a hairline crack in this vault of silence.

He tells me he's always been afraid that one day someone will make all this public. He says this to me, the only person in his family who regularly makes anything public, that is, who writes and publishes books.

Why should anyone be interested in the fact that, like millions of other Germans, your father was a Nazi, I want to ask, but I don't, because I feel it would be impertinent and disrespectful. At the end of the day it's about the Rang family, and my father sees himself as the last worthy representative of that family. As was customary in earlier generations, the family estate was passed down to him as the eldest son. The responsibility fell to him, as it did before him to his father, to look after Sanderling's intellectual legacy, to work towards the rediscovery of their strange forebear. Neither he nor his father really succeeded. No doubt Sanderling owes the fact that he hasn't entirely faded into obscurity less to the zeal of his descendants than to his friendship with Benjamin. Yet my father did several times endeavour to revive interest in his grandfather. And in carrying out those efforts, he always had the slight fear that someone could take an interest in the rest of the family's history. Perhaps that concern even held him back from championing the Sanderling legacy with all the energy required.

And now I come along, not an eldest son but a youngest daughter, and one without the right name. What am I supposed to do with this, with this Nazi grandfather? Nothing. Besides, he's not telling me about it so I might do something with it, but because for some time now he can't get it out of his head. I have no intention of doing anything with it. I wouldn't know what to do. A Nazi grandfather, isn't that something everyone has? Even for me it's nothing new. I already have one. He died shortly after I was born. He wasn't the product of a cultured bourgeois family. No one made a fuss or a secret about his Nazi past.

I don't wish to and won't do anything with this knowledge; what would be the point? I have no interest in writing the hundred thousandth Nazi grandfather or father story. But I tell two Jewish friends about it. One of them is called Pierre. His last name is what remained of Apatchevsky after Pierre's father, who emigrated to France from Odessa, had chopped up his name so much during the German occupation that it was no longer recognizable as a Jewish name. Pierre looks like one of the statues on Easter Island. The comparison makes sense to anyone who knows Pierre and who's ever seen photographs of those Moai statues, though unfortunately it wasn't me who came up with it but one of Pierre's many other female friends. I tell Pierre about my father and about the keeping silent that in his old age weighs upon and shames him more and more. Pierre is less than ten years younger than my father. Many of his family members were murdered. He survived disguised as a little Christian in Saint-Étienne, until at the end of the war his parents settled in, of all places, Vichy.

When I was a child, I thought there were no Jews left; I thought we'd killed all of them. We, the Germans. My own forebears, perhaps. But they and their guilt had, along with their victims, become lost in the mists of time. In my school there were no Jewish children or teachers. There might have been some Jews in the town where I lived, I don't know. The first Jews I met lived in Paris.

Why am I telling Pierre about my father's shame? Do I want him to understand that Germans today don't simply live in carefree prosperity? Did he ever suggest that was what he thought? Do I want to tell him that German people, or at least some of them, bear a heavy burden because of what they inherited from their fathers? Does he doubt that? He's a very intelligent man. When we talk about these things – about what happened in the past, what is unimaginable but that we nonetheless must imagine – he begins to cry. I sit next to him, numbed by helplessness and shame. I don't cry. I'm ashamed that I don't cry. I can't.

In a book by Andrzej Stasiuk, I read these lines: 'I try and imagine a German man crying, and all I can do is chuckle. I can't even imagine a German woman crying. At most an immigrant woman with a German passport. Yes, the world would look a bit better if you could imagine a German person weeping.'

In my case at least, Stasiuk doesn't need to make the effort: I'm sitting next to my friend Pierre and am not crying.

Those sentences of Stasiuk's are pure hatred, that's what I thought when I read them for the first time. Or rather I didn't so much think as feel them like a punch to the gut. They are the most hate-filled and at the same time the most stupid lines I've ever read about me and my fellow Germans – for they have remained my compatriots in spite of the distance and even if I've often wished for different ones. Moreover, Stasiuk seems, like Hitler, not to count German Jews as Germans.

As a child and as an adolescent – and basically still today – I was unable to utter the word 'Jude'. It was a word that simply wouldn't pass my lips. What prevented it? Later, in France, from the start it came easily to me to say the word juif. My reluctance to say the German word brought together two opposing impulses: one was the awe I felt about the unimaginable things done to the Jews, the things we had done to them. And at the same time, there resonated in my reluctance something of the fact that in German the word 'Jude' was still an insult. It seemed to me that as soon as I uttered the word, I would have associated myself with those in whose mouths it was a curse. I was ashamed to say the word. This wasn't the personal, individual shame that someone feels who has done something unjust or ugly, but a kind of communal, all-encompassing shame that had laid itself over the German language. This linguistic shame, which lived and still lives within me as a diffuse feeling with no clear foundation, is something I've never discussed with anyone, so I don't know if others besides me have felt it. If others have, then perhaps it only occurred in my generation. How else would the expression *'bis zur Vergasung'* ('until gassing', meaning ad nauseam) have continued to be widely used in Germany well into the 1960s?

I've never talked about it with Pierre either. He's sitting in front of me, his beautiful face sculpted from stone, weeping. He only cries for a short time. It's actually more like sobs that he sprinkles into what he's saying. In between he continues talking in his lively, brusque way, and looking at me. I don't feel cut off from him. He doesn't look at me as if I were on one side of a historical gulf and he on the other. I'm grateful to him for that. With him I feel neither like a German nor like a non-German. As I sit there across from him, I feel like a human being.

I read a review in a French newspaper of the second volume of Susan Sontag's diaries. Susan Sontag, the most intelligent woman in America, if we can believe the reviewer, had a liking for lists. The best films, the best books, she'd read them all, seen them all. And as the supreme judge, she placed everything in a *ranked* list. The reviewer quotes from the lists of what she likes and doesn't like. Everything she imagines other people like, she dislikes, and vice versa. Among other things she doesn't like cats, paperback books or couples. She doesn't like swimming. The things she does like include office furniture, paying bills and watching figure skating. And Jews. I'm pleased to have a friend who's more intelligent than the most intelligent woman in America. I persuade myself that Pierre would never say or write that he likes Jews. But maybe he would?

I envy you, how lovely to have a house that belonged to your grandparents and that's still full of old family things, Gila said to me once on a train going to Frankfurt, where I had bumped into her by chance.

There is no such house in my family, no house that might have belonged to the grandparents and would be full of family things. I never knew my grandparents, but I know what she means. She's trying to say: Your grandparents remained unaffected, they probably even joined in, perhaps they helped to murder mine. For her, I'm standing on the other side of the abyss. I'm on the side of the fortunate bad people, she's on the side of the unfortunate good people. She's friendly to me, seems to want to be friends with me, and I believe, and hope, that I'm the same towards her. But I feel keenly that she'll always first see me as a non-Jewish German, and only then as a human being. I can't hold that against her. Do I nonetheless hold it against her? I hold it against my grandfathers that for decades – probably centuries – they created these abysses. As a child, as an adolescent, before I got to know any Jews, I already stood facing that abyss, and I always wanted to get to the other side. I always longed to be on the side of the victims (the fact that you can also belong to neither of these sides or to both at the same time is something I wasn't aware of). I can understand that some Germans born after the war carry out a transformation of their identity, inventing Jewish forebears for themselves and studying the Talmud, in other words using any means possible to make it over to the other side, beginning with self-deception. So are you saying you envy me my grandfather who was murdered in a concentration camp, my father who survived the camps and the death march and was marked by that for his whole life? Gila asks me scornfully. She doesn't really ask me that and certainly not scornfully; it's more that I imagine that she could ask me that. What would my answer be? It seems to me that the range of possible answers is fairly limited. Still, I could always say: I don't envy you your father and grandfather, but rather the conviction that seems to have grown for you out of their history, the conviction that you stand on the right side, on the only side worthy of a human being, of you. Or would you perhaps like to exchange your forefathers for mine?

The conversation never did play out like that, nor in any other way. After Gila's first remark – that she envied me my unbroken family history – I fell silent, feeling as if I'd been categorized (on the wrong side), repelled; not envied but disdained. But didn't a large part of what I've described, the categorizing, the disdain, come less from her than from me, who had assumed these impulses on her part and had attributed them to her as if they were taken for granted?

Will she, when she reads these pages, be able and willing to comprehend how I felt, how I feel? Will she assign me to my place on the other side of the abyss for good? Or will she stretch out a hand towards me? Have I stretched mine out towards her? I'd like to do it; I'm doing it. It's by chance, I'd like to tell her, that I have these grandparents and you have those; we can't do anything about that, neither you nor I. Common ground? Ground where we could spend time together?

I talk with Cécile about the burden of silence that oppresses my father. She and I haven't been friends for very long. I've developed a spontaneous, unconditional trust in her; it feels to me as if I could tell her 'everything'. At the beginning, I had a guilty conscience when I saw her; perhaps I still do today. I thought I could see how the past weighed on her soul and was reflected in her eyes. I learned about her grandfather, who was murdered in a concentration camp. About the annual trips she was taken along on, even as a small child, to the memorial service in Beaune-la-Rolande. I believed I could see how each of those family trips, each time they relived the day the deportation took place, cast a shadow over her face. But perhaps even here it was I above all who cast that shadow? And at the same time my guilty conscience came from the fact that, when I looked in the mirror, I saw no trace of a similar pall.

When Cécile smiles or laughs, the pall falls away from her face. Where there was shadow, now there is light: a warm light that shines into the room and is shared with all of us who are sitting there.

After getting to know her better, I was surprised and relieved to find out that Cécile feels more comfortable in Germany than in France. France has only ever regarded itself as an occupied country, she said, as the victim of the German invaders. Yet it was French police who were responsible for arresting her grandfather. Not Germans.

I almost felt grateful towards the French police. Not for taking him away, but for being French.

So I tell Cécile about my father's burden of silence and my plan to look in German archives for more details about my grandfather's Nazism. If I'm honest, it isn't even really a plan yet, more one of those vague notions that sometimes go through your head, and you think, sure, yes, maybe I should look into that, and then you don't after all, out of lethargy or fear. But now I've spoken the idea out loud, quietly but still loudly enough that she could hear it. She encourages me, strengthens me in my intention, which for now is no more than the beginnings of an intention. The desire to obtain clarity about my forefathers is perhaps less urgent than my desire to be regarded by her as a person who is bothered by the past. Not as one of those who claim all that has nothing to do with them. Or am I now making myself out to be worse than I am? As with so many things, the correct and the incorrect are inextricably entwined.

I'm conducting research. Now, after I've talked about it to Cécile, there's no turning back. I feel as if I owe it to her; as if I too must take the burden of my grandfather upon myself and can't be allowed to persist in my ignorance any longer. At the same time, the closer I come to realizing my plan, the more fearful I become about what I might find out. But I reassure myself with the thought that I'll only be carrying out these investigations for myself, and besides me and perhaps my siblings, they would be of no interest to anyone. Nothing would oblige me to 'make them public' – *someone* might do so, that's what my father is afraid of.

I write letters and file applications with the federal archives and the state archives of North Rhine-Westphalia; the former is the office where documents accumulated before 1945 are kept, the latter holds material from the post-war period. I'm astonished to discover that nobody puts up any resistance to my enquiry, that nobody demands to see any proof that I truly am the granddaughter I claim to be, even though I don't have the same last name as him. Apparently, anyone can examine any person's Nazi file, can even, if they pay for it, have a photocopy made. Under one condition: you need to know the date and place of birth of the person you're enquiring about. Since I don't want to ask my father, I find out that information myself after lots of rummaging around on the internet.

Both the German offices I have dealings with fulfil all the clichéd expectations I have about them: the staff work swiftly and efficiently, and they answer in a discreet, restrained tone of voice. Had I perhaps expected them to express to me their personal sympathy? 'Dear Frau Weber, we're afraid we must let you know that the grandfather you were so fond of...' No, of course the answers are objective and neutral.

But even with all this efficiency, aren't mistakes possible? I think of the well-known stories about mothers whose children were mixed up or exchanged on maternity wards. Couldn't that just as easily, no, more easily, happen with grandfathers? With people who now only exist in the form of documents and memories?

I think of the office that answered my query as an office building, probably not unlike a city council or courthouse: long corridors, suspended ceilings, fluorescent lighting, indoor plants, an exit sign. Kafka opened his novel *The Castle* in the Giant Mountains, a mountain range in the Sudetenland. I imagine that in the government agency that administers the Giant Mountains of Germany's past, the walls, as in most such buildings, are painted in pastel colours. There must also be people within these pastel-coloured walls, but I don't see them. When you write to a government office, you're not addressing people but a vast, nebulous structure, at once cloud and anthill. So I'm all the more surprised to receive a reply from a person who has a name. The man is called Jens Niederhut. I take note of the name, which sounds like a deliberately chosen pseudonym or the name of a character in a novel.

But if the reply hasn't come from an ant cloud and instead from a person with a name, isn't there some danger that through my enquiry I've already in effect 'made it public'? Or do archivists perhaps sign a confidentiality agreement, like doctors? My fear is absurd given that this grandfather of mine was only one among millions and nobody has any interest in him; still, I can't quite escape it. I search the whole online world for Niederhut, find him straight away, and sure enough, he has not only a name but also a face. The photograph shows a young man with very short dark hair, his shirt buttoned up to his chin, wearing glasses and an expression of the kind you put on for a passport photo. I also find one of his publications, on the topic of classified material in public archives, but my grandfather's dossier obviously doesn't qualify as the kind of secret file that would necessitate the 'security clearance of the applicant'. That's precisely what unsettles my father, and as a result me too. I hold a copy of the dossier in my hands. A dossier reflects a person like a strange paper mirror. I look at the reflection of a man I now have in front of me and try to make something out.

The man who looks out at me from these papers is different from the one my father described to me. This is also the first time he's looking right at me; it's only a copy in my hands and not the original, but in the documents – the famous questionnaire the Americans had all German adults fill out after the war – you can see his handwriting, a fluid hand that leans ever so slightly towards the right. 'Yes or No' is the heading on the first section. I see many nos and a few yeses: NSDAP, SA, NSV (Nationalsozialistische Volkswohlfahrt), Reichsschrifttumskammer, Deutsches Rotes Kreuz (German Red Cross), Reichskolonialbund. He designates his work for the security service of the SS as 'voluntary', which is what allows him to put a no in the membership section. Some volunteering, I think.

I'm poring over this paper mirror with the not unpleasant feeling that I'm doing something forbidden: my father, whom I've told nothing about this, would, I think, disapprove of my sticking my nose in these matters. At the same time there's the shameful feeling that I'm surprising someone in the hour of his deepest humiliation.

He's lying on the ground in front of the American victor, the one who humiliated him; he doesn't know that the words he writes down will be preserved for decades and that years later other people not yet born, strangers to him, will read them. The man looking back at me from the paper mirror is a humiliated person filled with shame, and towards that person I can feel – perhaps more than towards any other version of himself in the course of his life – a definite, albeit transient, closeness.

I see the terrifying names and symbols: the wreath in the talons of the eagle facing to the right and within it the cross, also facing right; the application for membership of the German National Socialist party in Munich, Braunes Haus, in which the applicant (PhD) testifies among other things that he is 'of German origin and free of Jewish or coloured elements', and promises 'to support the party with all my strength as a loyal follower of the Führer'. Cost: three Reichsmarks.

I'm surprised by how much closer to me these things are getting. How little about a person is captured in a file like this. And how much that small amount allows you to guess, or how much I believe I can guess. Height: 1.82 metres. Weight: 58 kilos. Hair colour: dark brown, eye colour: brown. Distinguishing features: appendectomy scar. Joined the Party in 1937 and left it again in October 1944. Member of the SA between May 1934 and June 1938. Rottenführer. In 1918, Iron Cross second class for bravery. The man who appears in the file states that in the elections in November 1932 and March 1933, he voted SPD (Social Democratic Party), and that in April 1933 the National Socialist mayor of the city of Cologne placed him 'on administrative leave with immediate effect and indefinitely' from his librarian position and then transferred him for disciplinary reasons. 'The reversal of the leave occurred only after many weeks of efforts on my part.' It does, however, emerge from his listing of sources of income that his salary from 1931, when he was the city librarian of Cologne, to 1945, when he had been promoted to director of the public library in Bielefeld, continually rose, from 7,200 to 10,000 Reichsmarks.

Involuntarily, I find myself assembling a complete person from these fragments, yet I'm aware that what I'm sketching is a phantom image. That picture is based on the two or three things I've managed to get my father to tell me about his father, onto which the mirror image from the file is now being superimposed. The man I see vaguely outlined before me didn't feel drawn to the yelling hordes, or only a little. A Stefan George type is how my father described him, with chin-length hair, not in the least a military man. I have to make an effort to imagine a Stefan George type who votes for the SPD, but if people can embody contradictions, why can't their phantom images do the same? When the leaders of the mob came to power and he was threatened with being driven out of his professional career path, he bowed to the new demands and, out of weakness and convenience, ate crow before those leaders. That's how it may have been. The fact that he didn't join the Party until 1937 can be explained by the fact that the Party didn't accept new members between summer 1933 and 1937. Instead, in 1934 he joined the SA (Sturmabteilung), shortly before what's known in English as the Night of the Long Knives, that is, the purge of the SA, which may well have suited the phantom image; he was probably not aiming to stand out within a powerful organization but rather to be regarded as a supporter of the movement and otherwise to be left in peace. And indeed he didn't make it any higher up than Rottenführer, the lowest rank you could attain in the SA. Each 'Rotte' consisted of four to eight men. So he would have regularly worn the SA's brown breeches and shirt, with the red armband on his left sleeve and the brown cap on his head, fastened with a strap under the chin. He offered his services as much as was necessary for him to keep his job and to climb the ranks in his profession. In June 1938 he leaves the SA. Now he's a member of the Party and clearly no further engagement is required of him. Again he gets lucky with the date: a few months after he leaves the SA, the worst pogroms of these years take place. The SA murders, destroys, burns synagogues and shops to the ground. He takes no part in it. Or at least the dates permit you to hope he didn't.

It's only in later years that the phantom image grows blurry. A point arrives when opportunism and inner conviction can no longer be clearly distinguished. WARNUNG! SORGFÄLTIG DURCHLESEN! it says on the Military Government of Germany's questionnaire dated 1 January 1946: 'WARNING! READ CAREFULLY!'

The German text goes on to say 'Answer each question precisely! Answer questions "yes" or "no"! In cases where a question cannot be answered "yes" or "no", definite statements must be made, e.g. "none" or "inapplicable".' But what if no definite statements can be made? What if that person doesn't feel definite about anything? To the question 'Were you just a follower, or a devoted supporter?', which doesn't appear in the questionnaire, the man to whom it ought to be directed would himself quite possibly be unable to provide a definite answer. At some point, it seems the opportunist turned – perhaps precisely in order to no longer be an opportunist – into the ardent Nazi my father knew. I read *The Captive Mind* by Czesław Miłosz. All human behaviour, Miłosz writes, contains an element of acting. After lots of practice, a person comes to identify with their role so much that in the end they can no longer distinguish their old self from the character they're portraying. The trickery of the acting that aims to pull the wool over the eyes of those in power provides the person who practises it with a feeling of superiority and satisfaction, indeed of enjoyment, according to Miłosz, for it allows the person to see in their opposite a fool they disdain, a dangerous animal that they're rendering harmless. In reality, however, the person is falling into their own trap.

Between 1942 and 1944, the phantom image states that he was 'voluntary cultural correspondent' for the security service of the SS and that in this role he drew up 'reports on the functioning and problems of the library system, the book trade, literature, theatre, film and related cultural realms'. 'The functioning and problems of the library system' sounds positively innocuous. But why would the SS security service have been interested in something so innocuous? Publications of all kinds were vetted for their ideological suitability by 'voluntary' contributors. And the classification of books went hand in hand with the classification of human beings.

The Jewish friends of his father – that is, of the man I'm calling Sanderling – had for some time no longer been in Germany; some of them (Benjamin) were no longer alive. I was able to take a look at the letters that Erich and Lucie Gutkind wrote from exile to Sanderling's widow Emma. 'Dearest Emma!' many of them begin, or 'My dear ones!' The two of them wrote with fervent, heart-rending affection: for Emma, for a Germany that had vanished, and for their own world, which had been ripped away from them forever.

In an early letter sent in 1933 from The Hague while they were still emigrating, Erich Gutkind writes to Sanderling's widow and one of her sons: 'The geographical separation, painful though it is, isn't the worst part. But there's a sinister wall between those inside and those outside, which language can't really penetrate. It shouldn't be that way. We have to forever remain truly close to and clear with one another. We love you very much. You're among the people we cherish the most. You're our most marvellous and most deeply felt memory. You will always understand us. We don't fear anything. Not even a wall.'

In a later letter, the two emigrants implore Emma's son B. – my father's father, the phantom image – to send them a few lines. By then he was walking the streets of Bielefeld with his SA platoon.

Added as an appendix to the questionnaire he filled out for the Americans there's a list of his publications and lectures. As early (or as late) as 1933 he wrote an essay about Kafka; another one from 1934 is entitled 'The Proletarian Writer B. Traven'. A parenthesis after the title states proudly: *Printing was forbidden by the NSDAP!* He later wrote about Goethe, Gottfried Keller and, it must be admitted, Hermann Hesse. He gave talks on Gutenberg and on Mozart, and organized readings. The topics of the last few lectures he gave are 'Europe as a Family of Peoples/The Course of German History' (presented in 1943 to the local NSDAP group in Bielefeld-Königsbrügge), 'World View and Education' and 'German Easters'. The final one was presented at the 1944 NSDAP Easter Sunday celebration.

The documents appended to the questionnaire include all kinds of character references, including one written by his own brother, which contains various inaccuracies designed to facilitate his release. This brother, placed in a similar position by the country's new rulers, had submitted to professional demotion – from university lecturer to simple schoolteacher – and had not joined the Party. But the most important testimonial is a letter from Martin Buber. So, having got into dire straits once the war ended, my grandfather overcame his shame and asked for a character reference. As far as I can tell, Buber was the only Jew who had been willing to take a stand for this former SA and SD man (but did he even know that the supplicant had been those things?) whom he'd known as a young man before 1933. Generously, he wrote on letterhead from the Hebrew University in Jerusalem: 'Dr B. Rang, for whom I'm writing this character reference, is the son of my late friend Florens Christian Rang, one of the most noble Germans of our time. I've known Bernhard Rang since he was a young man and on the basis of that acquaintance can say with certainty that, while he may not have proven sufficiently steadfast in response to the political powers, he did in his heart remain true to the cause of humanity. He will undoubtedly be of use to that cause if he is allowed to be more freely active.' To be 'whitewashed' by a letter from Martin Buber: most people could only dream of such a thing. It does however become clear from the letter that the man who was thus white- or grey-washed owed it solely to Buber's friendship with his father.

A Protestant minister wrote that Dr Rang was by no means a political fanatic, instead that he had endeavoured faithfully to carry out his duties 'for the true benefit of our people. If he has completely changed his ideological position, as I've become convinced he has, then in my opinion that simply matches the sincerity of his being, which has always been a part of his nature.'

As I pore over these documents, I can't free myself of the feeling that I'm an intruder who doesn't have permission to be in this other person's life, this other time.

Have I made any progress? Do I know more than I did?

I continue my research, arrange to have excerpts from my grandfather's personnel file sent to me by the Bielefeld City Archive, including an application to the mayor of Bielefeld for time off: *At the command of the Inspector of the Security Police and of the Düsseldorf SD, I'm ordered to attend a training camp for SS leaders in Prague from 11 to 18 October 1943.* On 28 March 1944, the mayor of Bielefeld certifies that 'alongside his duties as head of the Bielefeld city library B. Rang plays an active and important role in the security service of the SS'.

In a book by Carsten Schreiber, I read that even the 'voluntary' members of the security service had SS ranks and owned SS uniforms, which they may have only worn on special occasions. Together with their family, they formed an SS clan. They functioned as 'the nation's intellectual shock troops' who had to be 'clean of character and beyond reproach as National Socialists and to combat the inner Judaization of German living space'.

I find out (from *Heydrich's Elite* by Jens Banach) that SS leadership camps took place in various places in Germany, but also at the Reichsschule for the Security Police and the SD in Prague. To get promoted to SS-Führer, members of the security police and the SD had to undergo an examination in this SS camp. So in 1943 my grandfather may well have been in the process of gradually climbing the ranks of his elite organization.

Because I want to make sure that neither the desire for revenge nor shame is leading me to treat my grandfather too harshly or too considerately, I consult the historian Walter Pehle about all the documents I now have copies of. I also ask him about the elegant Villa Klasing in Grünstraße, the headquarters of the security service in Bielefeld, where my grandfather lived with his family in 1944. Pehle replies that 'after all is said and done', my grandfather became 'unreservedly' 'entangled' (the quotation marks around individual words stem from Pehle, and the way I understand them is that these hackneyed words only inadequately convey what they mean). Finally, he writes: 'Dear Frau Weber, I would suggest that from now on you allow yourself no more illusions about your grandfather.'

I hadn't realized I still had any illusions about him. But I did.

Don't even the most cold-blooded murderers have to withstand the gaze of their victims well beyond those victims' deaths? Don't torturers have to carry within them for the rest of their lives images of the persecuting and murdering they perpetrated? Snitches get neither their fingers nor their memories dirty. They sully language. Their language can no longer be used. They don't notice. They don't bite off their own tongues. They keep opening their mouths and now utter prayers.

But am I not myself an informer if I pillory a man I barely know, as if I'd been appointed his judge? When all I know of that man is what clearly emerges of him from these files, or rather what becomes increasingly clouded in those files? That may be. But I swear that if I had caught wind of any manifestation of shame or of honesty on his part, no matter how tenuous and furtive, if I had come across the slightest indication of a tormented conscience in something he wrote or a conversation someone else might have reported on – I swear that in that case I would not have disturbed either his or my father's peace, or my own.

For Pehle, it seems that what characterizes and incriminates this man more than anything else is the apartment in Grünstraße. I think of one of my father's brothers, who as a seven- or eight-year-old lived in the villa with his parents while his older brother was already serving as auxiliary personnel for the Luftwaffe. And as if he's sensed that I've been thinking of him, as if he's heard my unexpressed request, my Uncle Ludwig, now living in London, writes to me for the first time in many years. He sends me a photo he came across in sorting through old stuff: it shows an attractive young woman in profile: my grandmother.

I ask him to send me more photos, I ask him questions. I play innocent. So am I guilty? Am I manipulating this uncle of mine? I suppose so. He readily tells me what he remembers, sends more family photos. I zoom in on my grandfather until his face is the size of a face and barely a hand's width away from me. I zoom in until he disappears into blurriness.

Two pictures reach me at the same time. One of them, probably taken in the early 1920s, shows Sanderling in a garden towards the end of his life. Branches grow out of his shoulders, like the beginnings of wings. He looks to the side, his gaze directed at a far distance and so serious and calm and penetrating that the viewer feels as if they were being looked at by this profile.

The other photo ('the ur-paterfamilias would be turning in his grave,' writes Uncle Ludwig) was taken at the wedding of a cousin in the 1940s. The veil of the bride, who is no longer a young woman, forms a large white puddle in front of her as if the dress is in the process of melting, although the guests take no notice. They look into the camera, some with a smile, others with a grave expression. Several men, including the bridegroom, are dressed in officers' uniforms, and the older ones wear medals, the bridegroom a (golden?) Party insignia. I can see my grandmother in the second row; behind her, on the wall, hang Goebbels and Göring, looking daggers at one another.

I ask Ludwig about his memories of the Villa Klasing, where the family lived above the offices of the security service. He remembers that they greeted the uniformed guards in the porter's lodge with the Hitler salute, 'but with the arm bent like the bigwigs did'. I hadn't previously realized that anyone besides Charlie Chaplin and his model didn't extend their arm when saluting. In any case, this memory shows that the children had the feeling that they, and their parents, counted as bigwigs.

Ludwig told me that he and his twin brother once trampled the crocuses while playing in the villa's garden, which was like a park, and were admonished by the head of the security service. One, two, three, no more pretty flowers to see, he told them.

And his father told him that once, at a reception, he had stood back to back with Himmler. That was the only thing he ever told him about that time.

Back to back. Why had he revealed this episode in particular? While he was standing there chatting, with a glass of champagne in his hand, he must the whole time have been feeling the presence of that man, his most highly ranked superior, like a branding iron in his back. He must also have felt proud. As if he had turned his back on a tiger in the middle of the arena. No, not a tiger. A tiger only kills what it can eat.

The next time we meet, I show Cécile the papers I've collected, and we look through them together. For her the most important thing is not so much what has emerged from this research as that I undertook it at all. That someone wanted to know. That they didn't let it go. That they didn't remain indifferent and disengaged. I realize with amazement that it's actually no more than she expects from Germans of whatever generation and similarly from French people – and what she has clearly encountered much less often from the latter than from the former. I'm glad to have fulfilled her expectations. And at the same time I'm not sure I would have embarked on this investigation if it hadn't been for her. Following her suggestion, I read Ernst von Salomon's bestselling book from 1951, *Der Fragebogen* (The Questionnaire), whose many pages come down to a single question: How do you Americans, who have no idea of the suffering we've been through, have the nerve to demand that we fill out such a humiliating questionnaire just because you're the victors? The tone the author takes is repellent.

Cécile asks me if I plan to tell my father what I've found out. I tell her my father has grown very old and frail. Have I discovered anything he didn't already know? No, I don't want to trouble him with this. Darken his old age. Exactly, she says, you haven't found out anything terrible – in fact, nothing worse than he already knew – so you can tell him about it.

I stand my ground about not wanting to tell him. It's true that he probably wouldn't find out much he didn't already know about his father, but perhaps about his daughter, namely that she's been rummaging around in their family's past behind his back. That she overrode his concerns. And that she now will even be the one to make it public. Because in the meantime that is what I intend to do.

Although Cécile doesn't say as much, it seems to me that she's somewhat disappointed by my refusal, which she perhaps regards as a continuation of the long family silence. I get the sense that, in her eyes, if I don't talk to my father about my research, I've only travelled half the distance. But maybe I'm imagining this. She understands my wish to spare my father in his old age. And she can see, as I do, the contradiction in his attitude: on the one hand, he's oppressed by the long silence that lasted up until his father's death, but on the other hand he'd like that silence to continue and for nobody to ever find out the reason for it. If the silence is to be broken at all, that should happen within the family. Through him. But breaking the silence and wanting to know are two different things.

The only thing he would like to know, my father once said, the only thing he'd like to be able to read, though no doubt there's no trace of it any more, is the evaluation his father wrote about the books of Ernst Jünger. His father appraised published material for the security service, and he remembers that included Jünger's books.

In this statement I heard various things he didn't actually say. I heard: the worst thing for which my father bears guilt will have been evaluating books suspected of being hostile towards the movement, of corrupting the people and of imparting ideas considered dangerous. I heard: in this time of horror there were people who killed and tortured, who jammed people onto trains and constructed ramps to help them sort and kill those people. And there were others who busied themselves with intellectual activity. Who sat in their studies and read. My father was one of those.

The idea that a man of his father's standing, a Rang, would have given in to any kind of base brutality, even just to breaking windows, for instance, was for him beyond the realm of possibility. And it's hard to imagine even for me, who didn't know the man and have experienced from him only the incomparably milder brutality of repudiation. Since I never met him and know little about him, I think of my grandfather, who was born in the century before last, as a more worthy, more stiff, more archaic version of my father. For me to imagine my father mistreating or murdering someone is simply impossible. But isn't that also the case for those whose fathers really *were* murderers?

So he was a bibliophile, this grandfather of mine. Others murdered; he read. But what did he take away from the books he read? Did they shape his disposition and sharpen his intellect, make him more receptive, more open? Did they touch something ineffable in him? What did the books mean to him?

I open the only published book by him that's in my possession. It appeared in 1954 and bears the title *Der Roman* (The Novel). It's dedicated to his eldest son, my father. The first chapter of this long treatise about the novel begins with these words: *What is a novel? It seems a simple question. But often what lies hidden behind the apparently simple is what's complicated and difficult, indeed barely comprehensible.* I already want to stop reading, and not only because I can't understand how someone could begin a serious book, or at least a book they wish to be taken seriously, with this kind of truism. I sense behind these few short sentences a person who is giving himself airs, who has to puff himself up if the vacuity or the meagre content of his way of thinking is to fill the following three hundred pages. But I do read on. I make it to page fourteen. There it says: *In a genuine work of art, form and content cannot be separated.* I'm stunned to hear something I had figured out by the age of fourteen at the latest blared out here as if it was a nugget of wisdom. The next sentence reads: *Perhaps we will get closer to understanding the novel as a form and a genre if we examine its content.*

I can't read any further. Somebody here failed to understand the very platitude he himself just proclaimed. I quickly leaf through the remaining 285 pages. I see that the name Ernst Jünger crops up twice. So the voluntary work for the SS's security service was worth something after all. Something could be recycled from all that litter.

Perhaps this man who's supposed to have been my grandfather was simply stupid? For the first time, this disrespectful thought occurs to me. Not the kind of stupidity you ascribe to 'simple', naive people, but the self-assured, boastful stupidity of the educated, who at no point take into consideration the possibility of their own narrow-mindedness.

After the war he became devoutly religious.

Everything begins with a short circuit.

Back in Berlin, when I read in Sanderling's papers that long passage where he describes his visit to the asylum, I thought I could see a crack in the wall of time that separates me from him, and behind the wall a path that began there in the distance where my great-grandfather stands, and leads in a straight line right to my feet. Probably an optical illusion. But I don't know how I could at first have construed his narrative any differently. What goes through my head is the riddle that was posed to my father and now to me: how can it be that the son of a man like Sanderling, a Christian who lived surrounded by Jews and regarded them as his elder brothers, became a Nazi? There it is then, I had thought, there's the explanation. *Healthy people gave their labour in exchange for money to sustain those incapable of work and in a higher sense incapable of living, creatures whose relatives could no longer tolerate having them close by and whom all of us were too cowardly to eradicate from the face of the earth.* Wasn't it the mentally ill, those incapable of work, the deranged, who only a few decades later were the first ones to actually be murdered, even before the Jews? Wasn't the lethal gas tried out on them, first in trucks and then in chambers posing as shower rooms? *Why don't you poison these people?* How am I supposed to construe these sentences if not as a portent, as a bad omen?

The *Reckoning with God*, which had been brewing inside him between 1903 and 1919 and from which the account of his visit to the asylum is taken, was intended to be a reckoning with Christianity, with the compassion it decrees, which he found hypocritical and cowardly. He had recently read Nietzsche. Perhaps he had happened upon sentences like this: 'The weak and the botched shall perish: first principle of our charity. And you should help them to it.' But he had not read the speech that would be given by Walter Groß, head of the Enlightenment Office for Population Policy and Racial Welfare at the Nazi Party conference in Nuremberg on 1 September 1933, in which he said: 'We have all experienced with horror the way the state and society deployed their resources to care with compassion and mercy for criminals and mental patients and the insane and idiots and made millions upon millions available for that purpose, whereas at the same time there was barely enough money to provide a dry piece of bread for a simple, healthy son of the people.' He wasn't able to read and hear this speech because by that time he had been dead for almost ten years. Neither could he have known how quickly the correct or false compassion of the Church, his own Protestant Church, would change into true savagery. He didn't know that the very Inner Mission he had been close to would willingly participate in the murder of those they were protecting. And he also didn't hear that other speech which the leader of the Heilerziehungsanstalt (Therapy and Educational Centre) in Scheuern, established by the Inner Mission, gave in 1933: 'How happily did those of us who for eighty-three years have been working to carry out the mission of our saviour with feeble-minded and epileptic human children welcome our Führer's measures to improve the race, which are the prelude to tackling the evil from the roots up.' Karl Todt – not to be confused with Fritz Todt of the organization of the same name – is the name of the man who would turn his Christian psychiatric hospital into the staging post for the death camp at Hadamar.

Everything that remained hidden from Sanderling and that he could never have seen even in his worst nightmares, all that is now laid out crystal clear before my eyes.

Nothing is more dangerous than the definite feeling that you have understood something. Isn't the connection I see far too clear to be true? Can it be so simple? Is there really a straight (or even circuitous) line leading from the ancient Greeks via my great-grandfather to me? Isn't it instead the case that the only discernible path between us only came into being through my looking back? But to believe that, I'd have to disregard the sign, the short section about the asylum that I extracted from all the notes. Because that part seems to indicate the opposite. I can't disregard it, but I mistrust the sign that seems to me to build a bridge.

I read and read, in the hope that once I've read enough I'll no longer understand anything.

Furiously I set about undermining certainty; more and more, I strive not to think in terms of concepts like cause and effect, indeed, in concepts at all; instead I move forward in a zigzag of contradictions. Then a strange letter arrives: one morning, a large package from Switzerland is lying in my mailbox. The saffron-yellow envelope has been forwarded to me by my publisher. On the back, instead of the sender's address, the same initials are written thirteen times, like when someone determinedly initials a contract or a legal agreement. The envelope contains four transparent plastic folders or files, each of which holds a larger number of pages covered in handwriting, long letters written in flawless German, the first two addressed to me, the others clearly copies of letters to the appellate court of the canton of Zurich and to a Swiss hospital. What I have in my hands is a kind of fan letter, written by a woman living in Switzerland in a 'nursing home'. I start to read. Right on the first page I begin to feel queasy. 'Your book is a big hit!' the woman writes. She is referring to one of my first books, one from which I now feel estranged. Immediately afterwards, the writer of the letter begins bad-mouthing the Jewish people, Cain, Abel and Abraham. It's soon clear to me that there must be something wrong with this woman, and yet I'm still not prepared for the sentence that comes on the third page: 'Your book just confirms, supplementing what the Bible says, that the Jews have always been and remain until today the most unprincipled and wicked people on earth.' The letter closes with the words: 'And no non-Jew should be content to worship the illegitimate son of a Jew as their God! With warm regards.'

I waver between laughter and dread, though the dread predominates, not least because I see myself getting caught up in this mania and co-opted by it. I read the letter again. It's reassuring, so to speak, that the woman seems to see not only my book but also the Bible as an anti-Semitic pamphlet that confirms her convictions. So the woman is out of her mind and the place where she lives probably not a nursing home but a psychiatric hospital. I read on. The second folder contains copies of several letters written to Diogenes Press, sprinkled with quotations from the Hebrew Bible, which clearly must have published at least one book that corresponded to her world view (here too: 'A hit!'). That's followed by her correspondence with the court in Zurich and other authorities, in which she disputes the diagnosis of schizophrenia and among other things sues her doctor for defamation.

That's all very sad, but it has nothing to do with me, I tell myself. Or it's what I try and tell myself. But why have this woman's diatribes ended up in my mailbox? Now of all times?

I keep reading. In a letter to the Swiss doctors' association, she writes that her only intention is to follow Mosaic Law, for which she even learned Hebrew; in return, for more than a quarter of a century she has been irrevocably declared schizophrenic, excluded from the community and paternalistically held in state custody, which is tantamount to a death sentence. The psychiatrists 'fail to see that the patient has just as much right to his or her own value system as the psychiatrist does'. Why she insists on following Mosaic Law even though she has such a poor opinion of the Jewish people is something she doesn't explain. Why she's locked up, to what extent she poses a danger to herself or to others, all that also isn't clear from her letters. 'Fail to see': nicely put.

I don't know what to do. I'm angry because as always I believe things have meaning, and that I'm the person who's destined to find out what that meaning is. I'm obviously not going to reply. A letter catches my eye, the copy of a reply the letter writer received from some Swiss office: 'Re your letter of... with miscellaneous unnumbered attachments. Unfortunately, your case is not appropriate for our reviewing department, even though it was sent to us.' How nice to be an administrative office!

I tell Cécile about these documents too. When I mention the sentence that had so shocked me ('Your book just confirms…'), I'm not sure if she will find it worthy of laughter or if it might make her suspicious of me, but yes, she does quickly laugh and then I do too, and the shared laughter does me good. What am I going to do about this, she asks me once I've told her more about this woman and her letters. I tell her I don't know but that it seems to me this parcel is definitely connected to what I can't stop thinking about recently. Cécile replies that she's superstitious and that in my position she would immediately throw away the letter or destroy it. She wouldn't want to keep a letter like that anywhere near her. I can understand that. But I want to read the letter again more carefully; until now I've only skimmed it.

And now it's still lying there with other papers on the floor next to my desk. It's lying in one of the piles of books and papers relating to the thing I can't get out of my mind lately. More and more it seems to me that everything connects to that, which is why the piles keep getting higher. Might this letter bring me bad luck, as Cécile feared it might? Lying on the same pile is the film *Shoah*, which I've never watched in full and whose five hundred and fifty minutes I now want to put myself through as soon as I summon up the courage. I glance at the back of the case and the cover text which is in Dutch only – the DVDs must have been manufactured in the Netherlands. I read that 'Shoah *is een magische film over de meest barbaarse daad van de 20e eeuw*'. It's also '*een meesterwerk*' and '*een schokkende film*'.

The thought occurs to me that if the woman who wrote the letter hadn't been living in a Swiss asylum and instead a German or Polish one, she would presumably have been among the first to have been granted the so-called 'mercy killing'. That she would have been murdered even before the Jews she spurned and hated with such doggedness. Perhaps that's why, while I'm no less superstitious than Cecile, I believe I can go ahead and leave her letter next to my desk, confident it won't bring me any misfortune.

Perhaps it won't bring misfortune, merely a little bad luck? Unless it actually brings good luck? Just when I've finally decided I'll accept funding from the Robert Bosch Foundation if it's offered to me, I receive the rejection letter. In the meantime I've got hold of a book entitled *Muster des Erinnerns: Polnische Frauen als KZ-Häftlinge in einer Tarnfabrik von Bosch* (Patterns of Memory: Polish Women Prisoners of a Concentration Camp Disguised as a Bosch Factory). I read there that the company's own concentration camp, located in a Berlin suburb not far from Wannsee, was situated on the edge of the factory grounds, that the detainees barely came into contact with the other forced labourers, and that they had to work twelve-hour night and day shifts and were guarded by female SS wardens. That they were housed in the basement of an enormous factory building with water running down the walls. That they received slightly more to eat than they previously had in Ravensbrück. And that the turnover of the Dreilinden branch of Bosch in Kleinmachnow, which produced arms for the German Luftwaffe, mainly with the help of forced labourers, increased between 1938 and 1942 from 700,000 to 33 million Reichsmarks. Finally, I learned that the Bosch company belatedly – though at some point nonetheless – paid more into the German economy's compensation fund than they were legally obliged to.

So everything's fine?

In the book about the sham Bosch factory I also read the foreword by Ise Bosch, granddaughter of Robert Bosch. She writes about everything that is then described in detail in the book: imprisonment of Bosch workers in concentration camps, the death march, the decades-long refusal 'on the German side', that is, by the company, to admit to the crimes that were committed. She writes about it in the same way anyone else would, someone who didn't bear the name Bosch. As if she has nothing to do with it. Only the name and in one place the words 'in my grandfather's lifetime' indicate that she is connected to what happened.

But did she have something to do with it? Isn't thinking about it that way precisely what my French travelling companion not long ago rejected because it entailed holding all family members responsible for a crime committed by one of them?

Ise Bosch does, however, appear very much to feel that she's got something to do with 'that', otherwise she wouldn't have chosen the name Dreilinden for one of the charitable foundations she set up. The foundation's home page does not, as far as I can tell, explain what the name refers to. You can read what the organization's aim is: 'Dreilinden supports women, girls, and individuals whose sexual orientation and gender identity do not correspond with social norms.' Although this appears to suggest that women and girls are not individuals, in fact for the foundation they are the most superior and certainly most important individuals. The use of the name Dreilinden for any charitable cause whatsoever irritates me to no end. It's the name of a weapons factory which incorporated a concentration camp. Would anyone think of naming a charitable foundation Buchenwald?

Ise Bosch also founded a network for heiresses. There are many questions heiresses ask themselves that poor devils don't: How do I invest my money? How do I deal with the banks? How can I use what I don't need to help poor devils? The question of whether it's right to accept an inheritance earned through the work of forced labourers and the concentration camp internees is not posed. It's the same question I asked myself as an applicant for a grant from the Bosch Foundation.

It looks as if I've got lucky once again: my application has been turned down. If it hadn't been I'd certainly have taken the money, as Ise Bosch did. I consider including an acknowledgement of the kind that ordinarily appears in a book, but one that would read 'The author wishes to thank the Robert Bosch Foundation for not supporting her in this writing project.'

It's curious: since I set out on the journey towards my great-grandfather, the mountain keeps stretching out further and further between us and doesn't let me near him. I'm on my way! I want to shout to him. I'm coming!

It's not a mountain that can be crossed. It does drift out of sight for a few moments, but then all at once it's there again. It looms up where just before there was a flat surface. The sea. I have to think of that evening, not too long ago – though it was before I departed on my journey into the past – when I was sitting in a hut on the beach, on that stretch of Normandy coast where I'm now spending months writing and reading. There's a simple cafe there. Mussels with fries. White wine. On Sunday evenings an old red-haired Irishman (Jersey is within sight) sits at the piano. On this evening he was as usual playing a mixture of old hits, Piaf and Aznavour songs, and other piano bar music. I looked out over the water, which had retreated, the sun still shining on it as it set to the right behind the power station obstructing the view to one side. I hummed along to the melody the Irishman was playing and more or less absent-mindedly wondered how I had come to know it. I knew it well and hummed along sentimentally, which fortunately got lost in the noise of the voices, the clattering silverware and the piano music. Then the Irishman took a break and sat down at the table where I'd settled with other customers (in this little place, everyone sits together at large tables). He asked with a laugh whether we knew what the last tune he'd played was. We didn't know. He laughed again and said in his shapeless French, as if his words were dissolved in whisky, 'It was the Horst Wessel Song.'

The SA song. How could that have happened, how could I have hummed along to that? At moments like that, Germany was as far away from me as the past. I was familiar with the melody, even though you never hear it anywhere. I even knew parts of the lyrics and they came back to me now: The flag held high, the rows marching close together. The SA marches with a calm, firm stride.

Could it really happen so easily? Could you without realizing get drawn into something you despised? You had to be alert, had to mistrust your own impulses. I thought about the tears that come to my eyes against my will when I hear a certain kind of sea shanty or a march, or some national anthems, like at the World Cup. Could you train your mind to display emotion only during songs relating to partisans and resistance and not during fascistic or Nazi fight songs? Weren't there bewilderingly clear similarities in the rhythms and melodies? The melody of the Horst Wessel Song, which became the battle song of the SA, dates from the nineteenth century. Singing it (or humming it, I assume) is just as forbidden today as disseminating the lyrics. I'd fallen into a trap. Still, I'd only hummed along, and I hadn't teared up as I did so.

Did I need yet more self-justification? In any case, I thought of a scene in Jean Renoir's *La grande illusion* that has always made me cry. It's the scene in which the French prisoners of war, in the middle of the drag show they've put on to pass the time, defy their German guards by singing the Marseillaise. A situation in which being moved is permitted?

I want to go back to Sanderling – but is it a matter of going back or of going forwards? 'We know of the past only our own past; we understand of what has been only what concerns us today; we understand what has been only as we currently are; we understand it as our path. Put differently, this means the past isn't something that is finished, but rather something that is becoming. There is for us only a path, only future; the past is also a future that becomes as we stride on, changes, and was different.' And: 'The past that's alive within us is at every moment rushing into the future, it is movement, it is a path. That other past we turn around to look at, which we construct from vestiges, which we narrate to our children, which was passed on to us as a narrative by our ancestors, that past has the appearance of rigidity, and also cannot continually change, because it has become an image, is no longer reality.'

I've pondered various conceptions of history, without being able to force my own thoughts and feelings in line with any of them. Yet in these lines by Gustav Landauer I sense a truth. This is how I understand them (probably differently from how they were meant): we look back and don't see anything that has passed by. We can't help ourselves from wanting to be transported back, from imagining, from trying to reconstruct. But however hard we strive to go back, in the end, willingly or not, we push what has passed by along in front of us. The two pasts – the rigidified, inaccessible past and the present-future past, which is always in movement – are two illusions that depend on and cannot exist without each other.

In 1914, Gustav Landauer belonged to a 'pneumatic' community. Pneumos: wind, breath, spirit. A hundred years later, pneumatics had become nothing more than a matter of compressed air. One member of the Pneumatic Collective of 1914, Martin Buber, wrote that it had set out to 'unhinge the world'. Theodor Däubler, Gutkind and Sanderling also belonged to the group. Eight men in all. The little collective only ever had a single meeting. Even the name Forte Circle, by which the group is known today, if at all, expresses – involuntarily – a utopian ideal, for Forte dei Marmi, on the Ligurian coast, is where the second meeting, which never happened, was due to take place. The group bears the name of a town that most of the members of the little collective probably never saw for themselves. It stands for an aspiration, something never attained. The First World War intervened.

Those invited to this second utopian meeting were to include, besides the existing members of the group, Upton Sinclair, Ezra Pound, Rabindranath Tagore, Romain Rolland and Rilke. Even one Chinese person figured on the list. And not the Emperor of China – he had recently been obliged to abdicate – but the first president of the Chinese Republic, Sun Yat-sen.

How did my great-grandfather end up in this assembly? As a man with delusions of grandeur among some truly great men? He had published, in the *Preußische Jahrbücher*, one essay on *Don Quixote* and a second on Kleist. And now he's ready to join Pound, Buber and Tagore in unhinging the world?

A few years later, Benjamin will get annoyed at the self-assurance of his friend Sanderling, at his 'peremptory tone, utterly dictatorial or imposing'. But who would adopt such a tone if not a deeply insecure person? And who besides such a deeply insecure person, one who came across as supremely self-assured, would have the idea of wanting to unhinge the world?

Of the eight members of the circle, five are German, three of them Jews. Sanderling, the Teuton, feels that's too many Jews, proportionally. In imagining this scene, I try to think away the giant mountain, to push it out of my field of vision. Sanderling doesn't need to think anything away; as one who shared in the mercy of an early death, in raising the objection he's to some degree innocent. Buber contradicts him, although 'such considerations weren't foreign to him'. His beard is still dark, perhaps streaked with lighter parts; it covers the bottom half of his face like a veil and draws attention to his eyes, his forehead. They look right at each other.

In their verbal duel, which I imagine not as heated but as serious and deliberate, each of them embodies his own religion. Neither emerges victorious from this struggle between Christianity and Judaism. Sanderling speaks of a Jewish characteristic that consists *of only being able to grasp profound reality by means of intelligence, without also being able fully to feel it*, as only Christians could. Conversely,

Buber believes that as a Jew, he has an advantage over Christians: 'I don't remember how I came to talk about Jesus and about how we Jews know Him from the inside in a particular way, namely in the motives and impulses of His Jewishness, something that remained inaccessible to the peoples subordinated to Him. "In a particular way that remained inaccessible to you" – that's what I said directly to the former pastor. He stood up, I also stood up, we looked each other in the heart of the eye. "It has sunk," he said, and we exchanged the holy kiss in front of all the others.'

In both of them, the Christian and the Jew, the feeling of being different and superior, but that feeling falls away – 'sinks'. In the end, one human being stands before another.

I can sense the gravity of the occasion, the intensity of this encounter. It's impossible for me to imagine Sanderling as anything other than grave and intense. No doubt he did laugh from time to time. But it's a profoundly serious and impassioned man who looks at me from deep in the past. The opposite of laughter as we know it today isn't weeping but passion. And indeed, the only laughter that Sanderling pays attention to is a passionate and gruesome kind. *Let us put our ear to the ground: from the rushing of the current of passion and glowing, we will hear a jolt, a cramp, a shout – a hideous laugh: the breakthrough of humans' derisive laughter.*

It's the laughter of carnival. Anyone who associates carnival with amusement, masquerade and confetti would not merely be on the wrong track but at precisely the opposite pole from that which is examined in Sanderling's *Historischer Psychologie des Karnevals* (Historical Psychology of Carnival). The carnival being dealt with here, the Greek cult of Dionysus, has more in common with tragedy than with any kind of joking or gaiety. Here it's about giving yourself over to *cannibalistic bloodthirstiness*. Women tear off the flesh of sacrificial animals – most often a bull embodying the god Dionysus himself – with their teeth. Mothers rip little children apart, one limb after another, and eat them. That's the kind of laughter my great-grandfather took pleasure in! A gruesome, bestial laughter that scorns God and humanity. *Baring their teeth at the Gods, they laugh at deicide.*

I read the book with amazement and repeatedly with horror. Up to a certain point, I can follow its author, such as when he finds in the history of laughter *a history of growing harmlessness*. I recognize how harmless the laughter we present-day people call 'subversive' is compared with the barbaric, crazed laughter of the Babylonians he describes. The desire for frenzy, lawlessness, dissolution of boundaries, the rejection of reason, sobriety and scepticism: perhaps I can sense where they might be based in him, yet my anxiousness and trepidation – and not least the giant mountain that rises up between us – prevent me from fully comprehending his fascination for currents of passion and intensity. For this isn't to him the distant past or a dead object of study. The roaring inside him, he wants us to understand, was for a long time only faintly perceptible, yet it never stopped altogether. Now he can hear it getting stronger and stronger.

Reading this book, which he wrote in 1909 and then revised without weakening after the First World War, makes me ill at ease. That war was not yet the last great carnival.

It's as if I'm reading a medical examination of the state of the nation. The illness (a dangerous epidemic) hasn't yet properly broken out, but the first frightening symptoms can certainly be detected. The doctor carrying out the study has himself fallen victim to it. And the most peculiar thing is that he seems to want to foster rather than restrict the spread of the illness. Yes, he can't wait any longer for it to spread; that's how intolerable he finds this incubation stage.

Our entire condition seems to want to break out. Are we a birth? Are we an abscess? It lies upon us like a nightmare; we breathe in gasps, in spurts, oppressed, anxious; we suffocate in the pressure. And: *Our blood pounds in our veins, as if it wanted to break through the skin; all the old scars ache. In the places where breaks happened in the past, that's where the rush of blood breaks through if fever carries us away.*

The study tells us less about the origins of carnival in antiquity than about the situation in Germany in the early twentieth century. Like all books, it reveals much about the attitude of its author. *One day we'll break out*, he writes elsewhere. *We'll become patricides. Christicides-deicides-patricides.* By 'we' he means Germans. And by Germans he means Prussians. He exhorts Prussians to shatter the foundations. We're going to start again from the very beginning.

He's serious.

In everything he ever started and ever said, he was serious.

Frighteningly serious.

When God retreated from our world, He took seriousness with Him. Where would such a thing still be found? With fanatical Muslims, Christian sects, Orthodox Jews? Is its disappearance to be welcomed or bemoaned? Welcomed *and* bemoaned?

A few months after the holy kiss between Buber and Sanderling, the First World War breaks out. The two men blow into their war trumpets with the same seriousness they brought to questions of faith.

The world doesn't need them. It's unhinging itself.

I travel to Braunfels an der Lahn, where Sanderling spent the final years of his life, from 1920 onwards, in a small, simple house with pointed gables which he named In God's Ground. God never took leave from his life. He could be an enemy. A *swine*, a *scoundrel*, a *pest*. But He remained his God. Or did he perhaps rant and rave at Him so frightfully because he saw Him eluding him?

Today, Hecksbergweg is called Hecksbergstraße. The house numbers have been changed. I don't have a photo of the house, I know only that it was modest, only had one storey, and above all pointed gables. I see one or two that could be the right one. I take a picture of one house, from which a man emerges right away and asks me why I'm taking photographs.

The house that may well have been Sanderling's doesn't immediately evoke God's ground. The village rises up above it, and above that, the castle. Further above that, on this morning, hangs the warm summer sun, turning the castle into a darkly contoured backdrop which against the light looks more medieval than it perhaps did during the Middle Ages.

Yes, this is what a place of retreat looks like. Retreat from the noise of the city, retreat from a world of factories and crowds that no longer have anything above them, no heaven, no emperor, no prince. Here, you look up at all three, you might think. Retreat into a longed-for, unspoiled world? Into the past? Might In God's Ground be the name of a modest, pious contentment? Something like 'My cosy Christian home'? For a moment I almost believed it myself. Doesn't it sound that way to present-day ears? But no. Sanderling is as far away from contentment, even a pious form, as from the planet Jupiter. His In God's Ground has nothing to do with stuffy cosiness. With what then?

'As surely as the Father in His simple nature bears the Son naturally, just as surely He bears him in the inmost recesses of the spirit, and this is the inner world. Here God's ground is my ground and my ground is God's ground. Out of this inmost ground, all your works should be wrought without Why.'

The man who translated Meister Eckhart's *Mystical Writings* from Middle High German into modern German is Gustav Landauer: one of the seven men with whom Sanderling wanted to unhinge the world. Sanderling read Meister Eckhart's writings in Landauer's version and no doubt also in Middle High German; Eckhart's sermon *Beati pauperes spiritu*, 'Blessed are the poor in spirit', also had a profound effect on him. The 'God's ground' he means and in which he wishes to live refers to the deepest of all depths. His longing for a return to the past applies not to any unspoiled world but rather to an origin, no, to *the* origin. It's a return to a place where there was still no why and no wherefore. It's a return to a state in which a person, in which he, Sanderling, would no longer be an isolated, lost individual, where he would no longer be painfully cut off from the world around him and from God. In this state there is neither above nor below, neither outside nor inside. The origin, God's ground, is an all-encompassing unity.

Sanderling names his house after an invisible, inner place, one to be aspired to. I search for such a space inside me, but all I find is what today we call an 'inner world', which is just as distant from God's ground as is the outer world. Nonetheless, my inner world allows me to arrive at a *concept* of that God's ground, even if it's not the kind of image I have of the Garden of Eden or of Purgatory. To clarify for myself that missing space and the vast distance that separates me from Sanderling, I imagine that for a great-grandchild of mine, which I'll never have, love would be only a conception and no longer something lived. In my letters, which this grandchild would have trouble deciphering, in books and other writings from my own and an earlier time, they would read what used to be meant by the word *love*. They would more or less understand it, but they would no longer feel anything. For such a great-grandchild, I'd be as far away as a Stone Age person. And me? Would I even still be able to consider this great-grandchild a human being? Wouldn't all other words also start to falter? Is this so different from what has happened with 'God'? With 'God's ground'?

I read books in the hope that they will bring Sanderling closer to me, or rather me closer to him. Most books explaining the past contain information, but that information is lifeless. The content shifts imperceptibly, while the terms remain the same. Nobody notices that the content has withered and died out long ago. I'm startled when I try and turn my gaze back one hundred years. I feel like those old people who can no longer perceive particular sound frequencies, like the chirping of crickets, for instance. Is this how it works with the past too? Do we even still have the same senses?

Braunfels an der Lahn. I walk across the old village square, where the half-timbered houses and the defunct fountain have been neatly renovated and decorated with flower boxes. The cobblestones are freshly relaid. It's one of those towns where Germans like to pay a visit to themselves on the weekends. The old places hold a rejuvenating mirror up to them: here they can see themselves back in a state of innocence that has been lost forever. They enjoy the feeling that here the world is still as it should be. More than that: here they themselves are still as they should be. Why do I write 'they', 'Germans'? Why do I exclude myself? Not because I've already been living abroad for so long; even less because I wouldn't share their longing. But the half-timbered idylls have always given me the creeps. They remind me more of cosmetic surgery than of the fountain of youth.

In 1920 Braunfels is by no means a questionable half-timbered idyll. An old German town has nothing to make it suspect for anyone. Very near Braunfels, iron ore is mined. The mines belonged to the Krupp firm. Gutglück (Little Happiness) Pit. Würgengel (Angel of Death) Pit. I don't know if Sanderling notices any of this subterranean activity; no doubt on Sundays you would encounter miners in the alleys of the town. But I do know he doesn't only focus his attention on the spiritual and instead wishes to endow everything practical with the spiritual. He's the chair of the arbitration committee in Wetzlar, the next town over, which rules on disputes between workers and owners.

Under the pointed gables of In God's Ground, Benjamin and Buber are regular visitors. A journal is planned, in which the friendship between Christianity and Judaism will be experienced and deepened. I imagine that Emma, Sanderling's wife, has a girl who helps her in the kitchen. Sanderling is the opposite of an epicure. He eats because human beings must nourish themselves; I imagine that he doesn't even drink. He sits there with an intense expression, not even noticing the full plate in front of him, knife and fork useless in his hands. Benjamin is small and round. Their conversations revolve around Shakespeare, Hölderlin and the nature of translation. They talk of harte Fügung (rough jointing), by which they have in mind a certain kind of poetry and a certain way of translating it.

Braunfels an der Lahn is barely twenty kilometres from Hadamar. Another kind of rough jointing? In the state psychiatric clinic in Hadamar, between January and August 1941 more than ten thousand people were murdered, people who were no longer considered human. They were regarded as *vermin, ballast, empty shells*. On the way from Braunfels to Hadamar, I feel queasy at the thought that in travelling this route I'm establishing a connection. This direct connection exists only in the geographical sense, I tell myself. There's a road running from one place to the other, there isn't a causal link. Like between Weimar and Buchenwald? Or like others?

Why don't you poison these people? That question put to a doctor by a Protestant pastor, which I read in Sanderling's report on his visit to the asylum – how can I forget it? I try in vain to banish it by reminding myself that the passage in question, which I happened upon by chance, is probably the only one in all the writing Sanderling left behind that seems to point with unbearable clarity and brutality to what was to come. Seems to? Yes, seems to. For while I may have read what was written there, I continue to mistrust that apparent unambiguity. I have to know more.

So I'm travelling from Braunfels to nearby Hadamar. There too there's a castle. There too there are half-timbered houses. But Hadamar doesn't look like a place you would come to visit at the weekend. The streets are bleak and not in the least bit idyllic. Getting out of the car, I look up at a threatening, fortress-like building surrounded with barbed wire. Might that be the psychiatric hospital? That's what the former asylum became. But no, that's not what any psychiatric hospital looks like any more. A prison, perhaps? Probably both. One part of the clinic is a closed unit in which for instance drug-addicted burglars or violent offenders are interned in so-called conformity with the rules. Forensic psychiatry, it's called.

It's two o'clock in the afternoon, I'm hungry, and in the only open cafe I can find I'm served the thickest and most German (German, more German, most German) crêpe I've ever seen, covered with equally thick slices of mozzarella and tomato. The waitress, very friendly and very tattooed, can't give me directions to the memorial. She's been living there for forty-seven years, she tells me, and still hasn't managed to make it there. Always at the cafe by eight in the morning, and in the evening she's glad to be home and able to put her feet up. She hasn't even been to the rose garden, and that's supposed to be something really special. She insists on telling me how to get to the rose garden.

The memorial is part of the psychiatric clinic and easy to find. The sign points to the main entrance, which is also where you go to sign in. Inside I ring a bell to the right of the door. A young girl lets me in and explains where to go and what there is to see. I'm the only visitor. I walk down a long, bright corridor with colourful children's drawings on the walls, through the cheerfully humane psychiatry of today to the murderous psychiatry of yesterday. Then I have to decide whether to go left to the rooms in which display boards document what happened, or down the stairs. I decide on the stairs.

The gas chamber is a twelve-metre-square tiled basement room with two doorways facing each other on opposite sides, with no doors in the frames. You aren't allowed to enter the gas chamber. Not that I want to enter it. You can look inside. I look inside. In front of the openings there are ropes preventing entry, like you find in front of the expensively furnished bedrooms or music rooms in a prince's castle. The murders were supervised by doctors who stood, as I'm doing now, outside the door and, unlike me, looked through a peephole as human beings slowly and tortuously died. I think of two people I'm close to who, if they had lived a few decades earlier, presumably would have been murdered here or elsewhere.

The room is bare. A sign explains where the gas was introduced. Perhaps twenty-five or thirty people would fit in the room, squeezed close together. Within seven or eight months, over ten thousand people were forced in, alive, and pulled back out, dead. By 1945 it was fifteen thousand. I read all seven hundred pages of Ernst Klee's study of 'euthanasia' under the Third Reich. I know that those murdered included not only the mentally ill but also people generally classified as unable to work, or traumatized by war, people with epilepsy, later forced labourers from Poland and Russia who were suffering from tuberculosis. I know that, even before the Jews, the mentally ill were poisoned with carbon monoxide in buses and in gas chambers disguised as showers and that the same staff later continued their work in the large death camps. Standing in this basement, I have the following statement by corpse burner Nohel in my head: 'After the corpses had been incinerated, the remaining bones that had fallen through the rust of the oven were put in a bone grinder, where they were ground into a powder. The resulting bonemeal was sent to the mourning family members as mortal remains. Three kilograms of this meal were allocated to each dead person.' And I'm familiar with the statement made by office worker Hedwig Hackel: 'The formalin solution for teeth was kept in the room where I carried out my clerical work. It was a really unappetizing thing, since the solution was in my opinion not nearly strong enough to get rid of all the traces. The teeth dispersed an unpleasant smell into the office.' I know that there was a Christmas bonus for the staff in the form of portions of gold teeth. I know that in Hadamar the ten thousandth corpse, a man with hydrocephalus, was celebrated with music.

I stand in front of the blocked-off doorways and look into the empty room. *Why don't you poison these people?* I look at the black-and-white tiles on the floor. Someone has a thought like that. Then some other people come along and simply do it. Can a connection be extrapolated from that? Even if it might seem like there is such a connection, I resist the notion that there's a direct link from Sanderling and his son and son's son and finally to me, the child's child's child. And yet *healthy people gave their labour in exchange for money to sustain those incapable of work and in a higher sense incapable of living, creatures whose relatives could no longer tolerate having close by and whom all of us were too cowardly to eradicate from the face of the earth.* I can't deny it, those are his words. I also can't put everything down to the baneful influence of Nietzsche. But is there not a difference, I angrily ask an imaginary accuser, between a person who under extreme pressure, in a moment of terrible doubt – he's nearly forty and he's about to give up again on the belatedly seized career of pastor, a career he no longer experiences as a vocation but as a curse and a torment, a decision for which he'll be disdained by the circles in which up to now he has moved, by his brothers in faith who don't take life nearly as seriously – is there not a difference, I thus ask the imaginary accuser, between a person who, in a particular situation in life, thinks and expresses a thought like this, and murderers who are employed and paid to kill without feeling and methodically all those who need help or are merely weak, and grind their bones in bone grinders?

There's a substantial difference, answers the imaginary chief prosecutor. Nobody ever claimed it was the same. Yet must that thought not first have been thought before it could be put into practice?

No. The accuser has got it wrong. Sanderling respected in the madman an unhappiness that surpassed the usual level. *But the most inwardly impressive human being I saw that day was the insane Hercules* is how the passage ends. The sight of the mentally ill people affected him all the more deeply because he saw himself – an exceedingly endangered part of himself, balancing close to the abyss – reflected in them. *Ah, I suppose it had never occurred to my Father Hesekiel to wonder if he himself might go insane. His life had never been so passionately stormy. That's why, from the safe harbour of his own dark mercifulness, he regarded the mad people as poor unfortunates.*

Least insane of all, says the chief prosecutor, is probably someone who with a clear mind recognizes such a danger in themselves. Your Sanderling may well have been passionate. But insane?

He wasn't alone in recognizing that danger. '*Cet homme est fou!*': Romain Rolland. 'His spirit was shot through with madness the way a mountain range is with clefts': Benjamin. Is that not the thing which cuts him off the most from all those who came after him, including me? His desperate search for something to hold on to, his unconditional nature about even the smallest things, his seriousness, all of which border on insanity?

From outside, distant voices penetrate the underworld. I free myself from the doorway I'm still standing in front of, make my way deeper into the basement rooms. There's a board with an explanation of how the incineration oven that is no longer there operated. I look into another room closed off with a cord, whose brick walls are whitewashed. Apart from a concrete morgue slab with a drain at its bottom end, it's as bare as the previous one. The floor is also concrete. A high window lets in summer light. A memorial. Who can memorialize thousands of dead? Millions? I stand there breathing in the musty basement smell. Something of what took place here penetrates my consciousness for fractions of a second as a torrent of glowing images and feelings melting into each other, and a second later it grows cold again: concrete and stone.

I decide against visiting the bus garage that had been built specifically so the sick people who got out of the buses couldn't be recognized by anyone. The inhabitants of the area saw them shortly after rising into the sky as clouds of smoke. In the exhibition room there's an old photograph taken from the village in which you can see the thick black clouds of smoke, getting broader as they rise, climbing up above the building.

I look at a poster showing a fair-haired giant bent over beneath a large burden. On each end of the board he's carrying sits a small, dark-haired man. The one on the left is wearing a hat and looks not mentally ill but terrified. The one on the right has ears that stick out, a flat forehead and a blunt nose. 'One person with a hereditary disease costs on average 500,000 RM by the time he reaches the age of sixty,' it says above the three of them. And again Sanderling's words dig into my flesh: *why don't you direct your gold, your services, your working life towards the enhancement of lives that can be enhanced, instead of to the preservation of lives that can't achieve anything.*

The chief prosecutor is lurking again. He too has read Klee's 'euthanasia' book and thus knows about the evolution during the 1930s and 1940s of the Inner Mission which Sanderling was close to. He knows the words of the medical consultant of the central committee of the Inner Mission of the German Protestant Church, Hans Harmsen: 'We give the state the right to destroy human lives – those of criminals, and in wartime. Why do we deny the state the right to destroy burdensome existences?' He knows about the in-house concentration camp of the psychiatric clinic that belonged to the state union for the Inner Mission in Rickling, in Schleswig-Holstein. He knows that the Scheuern psychiatric hospital, another institution of the Inner Mission, was turned into a transit camp for those deemed ill, who were taken from there to Hadamar and murdered.

All this is correct. Nevertheless, there's no direct connection. From, let's say, Nietzsche, Darwin, Sanderling to the later murderers. Not even from a father to his son, never mind to his daughter. It is unimaginably more complicated and convoluted.

You can always make such excuses, says the chief prosecutor.

He's right.

But take the so-called mercy killings, I fling down in a last-ditch effort. The term was used by the barking man with the little moustache to decree the murder of all unhealthy people and those deemed in the broadest sense incapable of working. Would you therefore seriously maintain that I might never, in any situation, contemplate the question whether a person or an animal might not or must not be liberated from its suffering?

Unlike me, the chief prosecutor has not yet reached the end of his arguments, but at this point I leave him there and get into my car. Driving away from Hadamar, I mistakenly end up on the autobahn heading towards Frankfurt, not where I want to go. I take the first plausible exit and immediately see a road sign pointing to the Hohe Mark clinic. Without my wanting it to, the car has taken me to the place where in 1924 Sanderling died, at sixty, of spinal cancer. 'It's hardly surprising that even life didn't want to keep this eccentric in its midst for too long,' I read with astonishment in the work of someone who represents Sanderling as a 'man without a centre'. Can you die from the absence of a centre? What is the centre of a person? Is it good or bad not to have one? Is it better to be at peace with yourself, settled in your 'centre', or to spend your whole life searching tirelessly for something, as Sanderling did? Hardly surprising that life didn't want to keep him for longer – is that something you can think about a man like this? It may well have to do with his being my great-grandfather, but I bridle at such a sentence. He was well on the way to accomplishing something splendid, I maintain. But because once again nobody's going to believe me, I pull my trump card out of my pocket and call on Benjamin as a witness. After

Sanderling's death, he wrote that he 'did know the wonderful human climate of this landscape of thought: it was constantly the freshness of sunrise'.

Today the Hohe Mark sanatorium is a psychiatric clinic. Sanderling's grave in the Old Cemetery of Oberursel, where, in accordance with his own wishes, he was buried beneath a simple wooden cross bearing the words LIVES IN GOD, no longer exists.

A few days later I'm again visiting my father in the Rhineland. The stance he's taken up as he waits for me in the garden is that of a child who's standing unaided for the first time: legs spread slightly apart, leaning forwards, as if surprised that, with his head at a dizzying height, he can remain upright for some time. But for how long? I hurry up the steps to him. We sit down in the house. Soon I start telling him about my visit to Braunfels. I don't tell him I also went to Hadamar. He would warn me away from making a connection where none exists. I would reply: they're just two places right next to each other. He would regard that proximity as accidental. But so do I! I would say in vain. I simply wanted to go there, first to one place and then to the other. That's all. He wouldn't believe me and would deplore my whole project.

So I don't tell him anything about Hadamar, only about Braunfels. Still, he asks: What interests you about this Florens Christian anyway? (The name Sanderling is up till now only for my private use.)

He gives me a deprecatory look. In those years, at the beginning of the last century, he says, there were dozens of eccentric types like him. There's nothing special about him.

I ask why in that case he and his father spent their whole lives indulging in a veritable Florens Christian cult.

He tells me he's given that up in recent years. That it was fanciful stuff, what the man wrote in the course of his life. And that the enthusiasm for war, this hoorah-hoorah at the time of the First World War, was positively disgusting. He says in the end he's distanced himself more and more from that grandfather, as he did from his father.

So what does he make of the fact, I ask him, that Benjamin, who in general is not treated as some numbskull, expressed such great respect for him?

He can also be wrong sometimes, is the response.

I ask why he's going to such lengths to run his grandfather down to me and to dissuade me from my project.

Whatever is all this going to amount to, he wants to know.

We'll see.

And what exactly will we be able to see, he asks, now with undisguised disdain. (Perhaps also angry because he suspects I'm concealing something from him?)

There's a tension between us, a showdown. We smile at each other in a nasty way.

He says: You want to write yourself into the family.

In a calm voice that takes some effort, I answer with something that's supposed to be an insulting riposte but that's just pathetic. I'm losing points. Why am I wearing myself out? My father is old and ought to be spared.

He has a coughing fit that doesn't seem like it will ever end and sounds scary. Everyone, he says when he can talk again, has to die one day. Even you!

There's schadenfreude in his voice, the satisfaction of the old person who knows it'll be the others' turn before long.

My father returns to where we left off before the coughing fit: You were closed out of this family, that's your problem, and for your whole life it will remain your problem. He says it in a cool tone of mild regret, as if talking about some kind of congenital disability.

He would, I say to him, welcome any researcher from outside the family who took an interest in this ancestor who's drifted into obscurity. It wouldn't surprise him that someone was showing an interest in this passionate, riven person who struggled for truth and who was friends with Benjamin, Hofmannsthal, Buber, etc. In my case, though, the only motivation he will allow me is that I want to write myself into the family.

My father doesn't reply. The tension gradually sets in again.

Twice during this visit, I mention that I'm having difficulty getting access to certain writings of Sanderling's published in journals, and that his book on political philosophy, *Deutsche Bauhütte* (German Stonemasons' Lodge), can now only be found from antiquarian booksellers for a high price. I ask him if he has these things. Presumably he does. But he makes no moves towards loaning them to me.

I don't insist. I get angry about his mistrust and can also understand it, given that every day I myself have new doubts about whether I can even begin to do justice to Sanderling and to what lies between us.

As we do now during every visit, we talk about the silence of the post-war years and his father's 'aberrations'. Of Sanderling's four sons, he's the only one who became a Nazi. Not a bad average for a German family, I'd like to say to my father. Yet what does he care about the average; he's ashamed that the one who disgraced the family happens to be his father.

One thing that's indisputably proven is the guiltlessness of the oldest son: he was killed in Champagne in 1915. Another son, my grandfather's twin brother, had the sound idea of devoting himself entirely to botany; he always just sat bent over his pressed leaves and weeds, my father says, in a tone that sounds as if he's talking about a loveable fool. He didn't have a wife. He returned from the war sick with tuberculosis. Up until his death he lived with his mother, Sanderling's widow Emma. A few days later I will find, in the vast digital treasure trove, an article by this blameless man on 'the common pasque flower' in the *Zeitschrift für Rheinische Heimatpflege*. In an issue from 1939. The pasque flower belongs to the buttercup family, I learn, and its Latin name is *Pulsatilla vulgaris*. It has the shape of a six-pointed bell, but 'In contrast to other species of the genus *pulsatilla*, which have nodding blossoms, the blossoms of the genuine pasque flower stand erect.' The pasque flower is poisonous.

I can't help myself; I feel as if I've happened upon a brief character description of this man. At times a coward, but erect and if necessary poisonous.

The youngest son didn't have the good fortune to live entirely in the realm of plants. Like my father's father, he was fired from his job in 1933. But instead of doing as his brother did and ingratiating himself with the new power holders and joining their organizations, he remained steadfast. Having earned a position as professor two years earlier, he now remained a schoolteacher until the end of the war. If my father, who himself is a retired professor, says 'a simple schoolteacher', it sounds like a huge sacrifice, and I don't doubt that it was. Why shouldn't a person have ambitions? Why shouldn't it cost him great effort and moral firmness to give up on those ambitions? For a descendant of the Rang family it will have been a greater sacrifice than for someone else. As a person who accepted being held back at the level of schoolteacher, he will be able after the war to submit a character reference for his older brother.

That character reference is inside the file I'm carrying around in my luggage and that I don't tell my father anything about. Perhaps I would if I could be sure that in doing so I wouldn't irritate or disturb him too much. But I'm already feeling uncomfortable at the thought that I've even brought the file into his house. What would he think if he rummaged through my bag and came across it? He would never do that. But wouldn't he be justified in getting irritated? What has the life of a man whom I never knew and who never wanted to be my grandfather got to do with me?

I decide it does have something to do with me. *You want to write yourself into the family.* Anyone who's shut out wants to be allowed in. I remember that when I was about twenty-five, my father offered me his name. I declined to take it. Anyone who's shut out doesn't really want to be allowed in. That person spurns the society that excludes them. At some point this strikes such a person as childish.

I reread the character reference written by the 'simple schoolteacher' brother. 'Based not only on my knowledge of my brother's character and disposition, but also on the many statements he has openly made in my presence, I've always been convinced that he was never part of the Nazis, with whom he got involved in the false hope that he might be able to improve something, but rather that he was always committed to functioning as an educator of the people in a genuinely humane spirit.' He wanted as an educator of the people in a genuinely humane spirit to improve something in the SA and the security service of the SS?

Instead of becoming the director of a public library, he could have remained a research assistant in a library – the equivalent of his brother's simple schoolteacher. Then he would have avoided compromising himself. But remain a research assistant indefinitely? He had completed his PhD. His lack of Christian faith was to blame, according to the character reference provided by his brother. After the collapse of the Third Reich, he became very devout.

The 'simple schoolteacher' quickly becomes a professor again after the war. Professor of Pedagogy, as his nephew, my father, would later also become. Whether they were good theoreticians, I don't know. Whether they were good practitioners of pedagogy, I could only say about the younger of the two. Regarding the older one, my father tells me during my visit that one of his sons from his first marriage killed himself. He threw himself in front of a train in Lübeck. With his barely perceptible, ironic smile, my father adds that the suicide left behind a farewell letter to his father, beginning with the words *Dear Professor*.

Out of horror I smile back. A short silence sets in. Neither of us comments on this information. I don't need to write myself into this family, I think. I've been there, growing in the shade, for a long time. *Dear Professor*. I could have begun a letter to my father with the same words. On all the letters I sent him as a child, of which there were lots, I had to write 'Professor Dr' before his name.

Every time, sooner or later, we get on to the topic of class arrogance. So this time we get there via the mention of this gruesome suicide.

His class arrogance doesn't go quite so far, he says, as to hold it against Kafka that he had a father who was a boor who dealt in fine linen.

No, not against Kafka. But he might well have held it against anyone who wasn't a genius. On the basis of a person's conversational style, he would have judged which part of society he came from, and would have disdained him for his clichés and for his failure to use the subjunctive.

Can you write yourself out of a family?

Perhaps I've got it totally wrong. But I can't rid myself of the thought that his father's misdeeds might also have had something to do with pride. With a variant of class arrogance, on the one hand: I, a Rang, a PhD, am to remain nothing but a research assistant? But also with what Czesław Miłosz (after Gobineau) refers to by the Persian term ketman: the ability cunningly to conceal your true convictions. 'Ketman fills the man who practises it with pride.' He feels himself to be superior to the Devil, to whom he's sold his soul and whom he believes he is cleverly deceiving. Until he no longer has any 'true convictions'.

We're sitting at the Biedermeier-style table and looking out towards the other bank of the Rhine. The next day in Cologne I miss the train to Paris and have to wait four hours for the next one. It's a hot day, and the streets and squares are full of half-naked people. In the museum it's cool. Sanderling had already seen the paintings in the Wallraf–Richartz Museum by the time he was sixteen, in 1880, albeit in a different building, of which nothing remained by the end of June 1943. I've often come here; a few years ago, when my father still left the house,

I came with him. In the entrance there's a poster for an exhibition on Wilhelm Leibl and August Sander. In the past, when he still lived in Berlin, I often stood with my father looking at a picture by Wilhelm Leibl that he was particularly moved by. It depicts a peasant boy sitting on a chair. The boy's feet don't reach the ground. He sits awkwardly on the edge of the seat and doesn't know what to do with his limbs. It seems to me now that what my father was always most responsive to in museums was the human element. For the particular way a mother's hand rests on her child's head. How a hesitant, worried, feeling, dreamy person is revealed through colours and forms, more humanly perhaps than in their real living figure. The way that some painters make the human shine out of their paintings is something I learned from my father. No, I didn't learn it. He was a good teacher in museums. He never explained paintings to me. Looking next to him, with him, I absorbed something.

Am I doing him and his father and grandfather an injustice if from the beginning I see the dark, malevolent mass of the word 'Poland' hovering above their heads? If I don't detach them from it? Is this just, or is it merely personal revenge? And his nasty 'One day even you will die' – is that his pre-emptive revenge for this book?

The Leibl exhibition is closed due to water damage. I carry my questions and doubts, Poland and the German mountains into the darkened rooms of the medieval collection. It's pleasantly cool and quiet in here. I stand looking at Stefan Lochner's *Last Judgement*. Christ is sitting on a rainbow; a second, lower rainbow serves as a footrest. Flying around him are blonde angels clad in blue and holding the tools of martyrdom in their hands: hammers, nails, pliers, vinegar sponge. The tools of crucifixion. The damned take up three quarters of the painting. I study the bat-like figures of the demons who mistreat them and pull them behind them in chains. One of the demons has black drooping breasts hanging from her belly, another has a grimacing face in its abdomen and one each where shoulder and knee joints would be. Almost all you can see of the blessed is the well-coiffed backs of their heads. They have to pass through an extremely narrow door, beyond which they dissolve into a pattern of faces without depth. A large white angel stands out to me, tenderly putting his arm around the shoulders of one of the rescued blondes. Like two lovers they look each other in the eye, forehead to forehead. Above it all, Christ floats on His rainbow seat. He has turned his head away from the damned, His arms spread out wide. With His right hand He blesses some, with His left He curses the others.

I stand there looking; my thoughts are looking somewhere else. And suddenly, behind the old painting with the shining gold background, another picture comes into view, one it seems to have covered up. In this one too, you can see faces filled with fear. Here too, there's a person pointing some people one way, others another way. Those people are getting out of a train and being led to a ramp. On one side the ramp leads to death, on the other into a living hell.

I get a fright as I look at this picture behind the picture, this forbidden palimpsest – or what is it called if behind the surface of one thing something else appears? I'm shocked to have seen an SS man behind Christ. I wasn't comparing, though, I say in my defence. I didn't make an equivalence of one thing with the other, didn't even think about it, never mind make comparisons or reach conclusions. One picture unexpectedly turned into a different picture. It was probably the gesture that led to this overlayering, it was the outstretched arms, one pointing here, the other there, separating the good from the bad, the wheat from the chaff. The strong from the weak. It was presumably everything I've been carrying around with me for months. How many times in my life have I stood looking at a Last Judgement? (Always escaping condemnation for now.) I've never seen anything other than a God in human form who rewards or punishes us for the course of our lives, none of which has escaped Him. I see the faces of the martyred, distorted with pain, their bare arms stretched up to heaven, the lustful and greedy grimaces of their tormentors. I see how they're pushed in my direction, how they irresistibly approach me. Whereas those who are saved turn away from me. However am I going to banish the picture under the picture from my consciousness?

When I step outside the door, the heat hits me. At least we can still sweat, I think. And as people who sweat, we Germans can at any time be imagined as alive, without having to laugh or cry; as plump, ruddy, sweating workhorses. Work. Is that German? The question brings me back to Sanderling, who knew better than anyone all about the 'German soul'. If not, would Benjamin have called him 'the most profound critic of German culture since Nietzsche'? Deutschtum: another word that can now only be touched and pulled into the present with the help of quotation mark tweezers. One more word that along with its meaning got devoured by time and like Minne or Sünde only continues to exist to the extent that I as a present-day person still have some idea what people might once have associated with it. Behind my notion of what might have been understood by Deutschtum hide all manner of meanings. They range from the German population, German supremacy (for example in the nationalistic, anti-Polish Union for the Promotion of Germanness in the Ostmarken, later the Deutscher Ostmarkenverein) to the innermost essence of the German person, which is probably what Benjamin and Sanderling had in mind. Does work have anything to do with that innermost German essence, with this German 'genius'?

Sanderling, the recognized expert and specialist in Deutschtum, loathed the work ethic he saw worshipped around him as an absolute value. The duty to work and what he called the *Protestant imperative (work, earn the means to sustain your life – out of mercy, dear God provides heaven to those who believe withal)* were abhorrent to him. Not that he was lazy. But he didn't agree that the work ethic should henceforth be not only the highest but the only ethic. He explained this in a 1905 essay about Don Quixote; what Don Quixote has to do with this remains somewhat mysterious to me, but I'm pleased to find that in Deutschtum as understood by Sanderling, no high value is attached to work: *For what makes us rich and great inside is never work, never possessions and never earnings, but rather comes like a visitor, like lightning, as an accident, a brainwave* – like a visitor or like lightning: I'm happy to acknowledge my connection to a great-grandfather like that.

Might he have read Max Scheler? I for one did read a book by Max Scheler that appeared in the middle of the First World War, *Die Ursachen des Deutschenhasses* (The Causes of Germanophobia). Scheler was only a few years younger than Sanderling; both of them greeted the war with jubilation, hoping it would bring about a strengthening and opening of Deutschtum. There's one chapter in the book entitled 'Eviction from Paradise'. An image has, he writes, appeared to the people of Europe, the image of 'a new, remarkable archangel'. This angel lacks brilliance and charisma and dignity. He 'bears the imprint of a simple working man with good, coarse fists', who 'laboured away quietly and slowly, entirely sunk in his task, but with a consistency, precision and punctuality that seen from the outside aroused fear, even terror, and as if lost in his task, worked and worked again – and what was least understood by the world – out of pure joy in unlimited work for its own sake – without an aim, without a purpose, without end'. This hard-working German, whom Scheler sees as the forefather of 'new noble houses', evicts the world from paradise.

I've always been preoccupied with the thought that the future is waiting for us. That it holds events, incidents, manners of death ready for us, that though we know nothing about them they're already there and just need to occur. What is waiting for us will turn all our previous living and thinking on its head, throwing a new, never-seen light upon it. Because we have our eyes open, we believe we see clearly. We don't see what awaits us and will soon reinterpret and revolutionize everything that's taken place and been thought. I think I understand what Landauer meant: the past is 'not a chain of links following on one another, all of them except the last one standing still and firmly rooted'. All the links in this chain are constantly moving.

Had he not died in 1928 at the age of fifty-three, presumably Max Scheler would, as the son of an Orthodox Jewish mother, have been taken to one of those places above whose gates the words ARBEIT MACHT FREI were written in wrought-iron letters. He would have truly seen the German working man 'from outside', as he carried out the work of murder 'with consistency, precision and punctuality'. He would have been his material.

In the mind of a person looking back, everything is present at the same time: Scheler's praise for the German worker, the slogan above the gates of the 'Metropolis of Death', the German industriousness that hasn't diminished even today. The course of history, the chain of events, words and images succeeding one another: for the person looking back, they end up all collected together.

By thinking of them all simultaneously, he abolishes time. In his mind, time doesn't exist as a separation, but only as one of the appearances about which he knows something. He feels like someone looking out over a landscape from up above, able to take in its various elements, woods, fields, river, sky, simultaneously. He thinks he's surveying something and doesn't know that the vantage point where he's standing is his own personal one, to which no other person ever has access. As it lies there spread out before him, that landscape exists only for him. He's the only one who will ever see it. He himself has brought it forth from the few components at his disposal. There he stands and looks; here I stand. And I can't get rid of the dull feeling that outside my field of vision what will become present, what's waiting for me, for us, is already there. What's past is created by me. What's to come has already been created.

What's waiting for us?

Nearly a hundred years have passed since Scheler's book appeared. And the Germans are still hated for their work mania. Deutschtum, which at one time meant something like the deep essence of being German, became under the Nazis a Deutsch-Tun, a German demeanour, and finally, after the war, a *Made in Germany*. German workmanship. A seal of quality. Today, for the first time, I hear in that *Made in Germany* an exclamation through which we brand ourselves all over the world, denounce ourselves as criminals and murderers. Look, that was made in Germany!

Am I starting to talk nonsense? The past, that which in Germany is present as the past, is a spider's web that stretches everywhere, into all thinking and action.

For there to be something like Deutschtum, there first had to be Germans. But do Germans really exist? I mean, as people who are clearly distinct from others? Is there such a thing as a German *essence*, did such a thing use to exist? I return to Sanderling, who was convinced about the specialness of the Germans – as of the French, the English, the Spanish. What does this specialness look like? *We are a harsh people;* furor teutonicus *is no myth. We possess a certain fanaticism. It's the best thing about us. Without this wildness, which is greedy for the coming-together of the ideal and life, we're lazy bellies.* We've lost the wildness, or else it's been temporarily tamed. We've remained workaholics. A future German poet, a German Cervantes yet to be born, will teach us – will *grant us to know*, as Sanderling writes, to my delight – *that labour power is by no means our whole strength of mind, he will entice us into ridiculing all morals and all beliefs to those who wish to rule the ground of the soul beyond the aim of actions – and entice us into play and tranquillity and laughter in the unrestrained belief in the goodness of our nature.*

Thus work is not the only thing that makes up our 'German soul'. Unexpectedly, you hear here about merriment, about play and above all about the *goodness of our nature*: for all our wildness we apparently possess goodness. Albeit a goodness that lies beyond good and evil? Reading Nietzsche is still sitting heavily in Sanderling's stomach. 'Goodness' for him no longer comes from 'good'.

Nevertheless: I cling onto *play and tranquillity and laughter* and hope that Deutschtum can stick to those three and leave it at that. I carry on uneasily with the Cervantes essay, which strangely enough still revolves around the German soul. (In the background I see Don Quixote brandishing his lance, but the German windmill keeps turning, unaffected.) The German poet to come, I read, will teach us *the new love of humanity*. Love of humanity sounds good, and yet I'm not comfortable with it. Why *new*? And here it is spelled out: it's a *love without mercy*. Without hesitation, this invention is laid at Cervantes's door. (Now Don Quixote sets upon the flock of sheep, a massive cloud of dust enveloping him and the panic-stricken sheep.) It's a love *that liberates our actions, even if that means fighting, robbing and killing*. (Don Quixote lies on the ground covered in dust.) A love that licenses killing and robbing? In earlier times, he says, Cervantes helped us *reconcile ourselves half-ironically with the lack of greatness in our politically wretched age. Today we no longer need that kind of humiliating apology for ourselves. We are no longer funny to ourselves.*

If only we had remained that way, at least at moments! *We are no longer funny to ourselves.* Is that sentence a key? Deutschtum, if some such thing exists or did exist, changes. In some periods we are (a little) funny to ourselves, in others we aren't. In the time of the little moustache-man, any feeling we had for our own ridiculousness had died out. And meanwhile every complacent gesture made by that man, every stride he took to demonstrate firmness, every thrusting-out of his chest, every swing of the arms, every nasty facial expression, they were all the embodiment of ridiculousness. And would have been even without Chaplin. With each of his rolling 'r's we could at any time have had him slip and go flying lengthwise down the podium steps. Instead we listened to him seriously, indeed reverently. We were no longer funny to ourselves. I write *we* because it's not enough to have been born a few years later and moreover to perhaps have emigrated to not belong to that *we*. It would be nice to be able to simply say 'I'm not German.' I also write *we* because by that I also mean we human beings.

What occurs to me at this point is not a comparison; or if it might be one, then it rests only on a particular issue, that of belonging: didn't many of those who were persecuted and tortured by (other) Germans repeatedly say they had never regarded themselves as Jews and that it was only the Germans (precisely those other Germans) who did so? It's the others who determine whether or not you belong to a community and, if you do, which one, and it makes no difference at all whether you recognize or resist their classification. The others are stronger.

The others, by which I mean primarily the French people with whom I come into contact on a daily basis, see me as a German woman. But what do they have in mind when they think *German*? All kinds of things, a variable mixture of stereotypes among which only a few are things you would like to embody. But they always have in mind 'belonging to the people who...' I'm not maintaining that they're fully conscious of making that connection. It's more or less like if I was talking with someone whose father had, I knew, been convicted of murder. I certainly wouldn't have that murderer-father in mind every second, if we, let's say, talked about the underground strike due to happen or the best way to prepare fresh sardines. And yet he would be present; in the back of my mind, he'd be sitting there the whole time.

If I say all this to one of those *others*, they're eager to contradict me; politely and maybe also honestly they say, 'But no, you're imagining it, nobody sees you or any other young German person as the son or daughter of a murderer.'

I don't believe that, and especially not the 'nobody', but I'll accept it and assume that I just see myself that way and also attribute this view to others. A projection. Could be. At the end of the day, it makes no difference *who* sees it this way: that way of seeing is out in the world. That's what separates me, separates us from the others. And if today a Deutschtum still exists, if there is still something that characterizes Germans and distinguishes them from all others, then it would probably be the awareness of what was done in Germany, of that special, deadly form of *Made in Germany*. That awareness lives in all of us, whether they deny it – what was done in Germany – or want to finally be exempted from it and to not hear anything more about it, or make pilgrimages to memorials and sit in the memorials' cafes and eat cake, or study Judaism, or daub swastikas on cemetery walls at night, or never give it a thought. The awareness of it is something they can't shake off, any more than you can talk your way out of congenital heart disease.

History is something you're born into.

Some German life stories are a single desperate and futile attempt to free themselves from congenital heart disease. W.G. Sebald moved to England when he was still young and devoted himself to Jewish 'fates' (I'm placing that word, frequently used in this context, in quotation marks because it carries with it the idea of a kind of inevitability and necessity that cannot encompass the murder of millions of people). He abbreviated his first names, Winfried and Georg, and henceforth regarded Germany and German history from the vantage point of an outsider.

In Sebald's novel *Austerlitz*, there are two characters: the Czech Jew Austerlitz and a man to whom Austerlitz tells his life story and who in turn tells it to us. Who is this person who does the retelling? He's an open ear and a blank page: he's Sebald himself, his literary representative. Of course, no writer is obliged to bring their own person into play as anything other than a ghostly presence; on the contrary, elegance and discretion demand the opposite. And yet it is a special case when one character (made up of the people from whose stories Sebald put together the Austerlitz story) is the only surviving member of a Jewish family, the other (who hides behind the narrator) a non-Jewish German born in 1944. The latter appears in the book as a person with no history of his own, without origins. That blank space is filled in by Austerlitz, who for his part definitely does have a history and origins but in a certain way doesn't have a head of his own. Like any character in a novel, he has his head, and along with it his language and its rhythm, handed over to him by the author.

This isn't a judgement of a book, and certainly not a condemnation of its author. Who goes to such lengths not to be or at least not to appear to be the person he, without wanting to, was born as, if not someone who suffers deeply over his origins? Who with his thoughts and with his body cannot carry them, cannot bear them?

Deutschtum, if some such thing has existed in the past few decades and until today, would have to also be a name for the compulsion, in some cases the life-and-death necessity, of a flight from all that is German.

Once again I'm hunched over one of Sanderling's essays. It has to do with Kleist. In the early years of the century, shortly after his retreat from the profession of pastor and his return from the east, Sanderling gave a lot of thought to Kleist and to Cervantes – but actually to Prussia. He writes about the *despotic life force* of a state structure that was still *lying around* from the Lower Rhine all the way to the Slavic border like a *crumbling mass of land*. About the Prussian all-or-nothing: *Demonic indignation* and *wilful fury*. For my part, it takes some strength and no small amount of wilful fury to endure this renewed swelling-up of Teutonic furore.

Kleist wasn't there to regard the world with a smile, I read. True enough. After many millennia of reflection we're still no nearer to an answer to the question of what a human being is for. But we can be sure about one thing: no person is here to regard the world this way or that way. And hardly any people, including Kleist, will be able to regard it in the same way for their whole life, whether that's with a smile or with indignation. But where does this antipathy towards any kind of gentleness, any friendly amusement, come from? Is it the expression of the bitter seriousness of an epoch or of an individual? Both? Let us put Kleist and Cervantes aside, as Sanderling basically also does: he's not interested in those two but in Prussia, in Germany, in Deutschtum. It's his seriousness, not theirs, that drives away any smiling. *Joy in the world died off in the great rage*. What brought on that rage? Prussianness. (Prussianness seems to be a kind of higher Deutschtum, its quintessence.) Sanderling's great rage, which he attributes to Kleist, stems from the fact that Prussia doesn't yet have the grandeur that's been longed for so passionately, that this is not yet the yearned-for *new kind of structure*, state power. It's still not Prussian enough.

Seen from a distance, this great rage resembles the temper tantrum of a child who in the end has been denied something that was promised or hoped for. The great rage! A poem by Matthias Claudius comes to mind: 'So I don't want to live any more, / The light of day I deplore; / For cake she gave to Franzi, / But none at all to me.'

We instinctively see in any strong feelings, any agitation by those who came before us, the emotions of a child. We feel ourselves to be more grown up than our ancestors, whose tantrums and dances of joy we smile at from our later (we believe superior) vantage point. The outbursts of anger of this ancestor-child make no sense to us. With our affectionate smirk, we provoke the child to fury (or rather we would bring it to fury: the child is dead). We don't take his deep grief, his rage, his wailing seriously; what we consider a discrepancy between cause and effect produces tender or caring amusement in us.

In relation to Sanderling, I feel myself to be someone later, someone more grown up, in a way that doesn't feel comfortable to me but which it's hard for me to do anything about, just as there's no way I could slip back into the child I once was. It's a peculiar image: the person who stands before me, or rather lies on his back kicking and screaming in furious rage, is an imposing, highly educated man, one who was friends with Benjamin and felt at home among Greeks and Romans, with Shakespeare, Goethe and Dante. How come I am nevertheless so much older and more mature? The giant mountain buried my ingenuousness and childishness beneath it. I'm denied bitter seriousness, furious rage. Too much space has opened up between me and things, between me and myself. The safe distance of smiling that sometimes freezes.

The further I read in the Kleist essay, the more my smile of the all-too-mature wears off. I read about a capacity to *throw oneself into doom*. About a high art, the highest of all: *the intoxication of the Dionysian passion for death.* Sanderling's voice swells, outdoes itself in boldness and strength, and in the end almost falls apart. In a powerful crescendo, lunging from the drumbeat of one exclamation mark to the next, that voice hurls Kleist's supposed legacy at me: *The greatest pleasure for German men is to be the enforcers of fate, of a passion that wishes to have its freedom, of the demon 'will' that rules the world, a function of the will to rule that consumes the coal that ignites it.*

I'm starting to think I know enough about Deutschtum. I was taught about it amid lots of noise. I have an inkling of what I'll never be able to know about this vanished word: how it might have tasted in a child's mouth, how it might have sounded in a child's ears. I'm too old for this word. In it I hear 'mass grave'. I hear the silence after the fanfare. I hear the whispers of millions.

Again I can see a direct path from here to there, from the desire for doom and the will to rule to the German giant mountain. But I'm mistaken! I read on, fight my way through the thicket of time, and notice, gratefully, that the direct path I could see clearly a moment ago doesn't exist here either; it was a dead end that soon finished and didn't lead to any mountain, and even less to me. Certainly, for a while longer, just a few years, it can still be made out: Sanderling – not only him, God knows, but also Buber, Gutkind, Max Weber, Thomas Mann and countless others – falls into war rapture. *I've been mobilized, hurray! and I'll be permitted to take part in the field in this struggle of the most noble and peaceable people against the envy and vengefulness that wish to choke them – God be thanked.* At fifty he enlists as a volunteer but is presumably too old to be a soldier; in any case he doesn't work with weapons, doesn't fight in the field, but instead is named head of the V Corps in Montmédy in Lorraine. Shortly before the start of the war, the French opened the railway line from Montmédy to Verdun, and now that line is used by the Germans to deliver supplies to the front. *The world's clock has twelve long chimes to chime. But even the first one announces how it's chiming: hard! iron! invincible!*

Sanderling's *hurray!* is the high point and at the same time the turning point of his most abject period. It doesn't simply look that way from a distance of a century; some who enjoyed the same era also saw it that way, foremost among them the shrewd Landauer: he who 'behaves like a Grand Inquisitor and passes off his own wretchedness as a divine law is not German nor human nor divine, but a dilettante hiding uncertainly beneath a priest's cloak, internally at odds with himself and therefore presenting himself on the outside as self-confident and imperious'. Well aimed, cry the French from their trench: that hits the mark. A penetrating psychological portrait, a thoroughly accurate characterization. Which, however, only applies to half of Sanderling. For he's a Janus figure. That's shown by the surviving descriptions of his personality.

He resembles one of those pictures in which, depending on how you look at it, you can make out either a rabbit's or a duck's head. But unlike with the Janus figure, with Sanderling both rabbit and duck can be seen simultaneously. They don't, like Dr Jekyll and Mr Hyde, always go out one at a time, 'and thus it can come about that someone who by nature has benevolent feelings misuses the language of his reason for the absolute most evil and presumptuous ends.' That too was written by Landauer.

It is without doubt the most banal thing in the world to say that every person and every thing has this side and that side and can be seen like this or like that. But with Sanderling, the two halves of his being diverge far more than typically happens. And probably further than any person can withstand.

Woken up from a dream. From a frenzy. As early as the first days of January 1915, he comes to with a bad hangover – comes back to his other 'self'. This isn't the kind of hangover that passes. A few weeks later, his eldest son Wilhelm dies in Champagne.

In this war, I've got two men on my conscience. One was a swineherd I not only suspected, on the basis of a perhaps incorrect tip two of my policemen had brought me, but also shouted at rashly and without consideration and calm and with words and gestures – I waved my riding crop around in front of his face – to get him to confess what he knew; afterwards, because nightfall interrupted the interrogation, I had to have him locked up until morning: when he was found – he was thought to be somewhat simple – he was hanging and dead.

The other is my eldest son. There was something in me – and not a small amount – that demanded his death. That reproached itself, as if this were cowardly and too eager for happiness, for hoping I would be able to hug him to my chest again, healthy and crowned with glory. Something that forced itself into this sacrifice, as Abraham did with his son. But to express it without idealizing comparison: something that inflicted cruelty on myself and him.

There's something peculiar about the words that resonate over to us from the past. They're the words of someone long dead, but how much warm life is still in them! Not long ago he stood before me in full armour and was having bells rung all round the world. Now all the iron has fallen away from him. The fire that flared up to the point of insanity now only glows gently. For the first time, I could speak to him. Could whisper something like 'My dear old great-grandfather'.

The most peculiar thing of all, though, is that the time has gone. That mass of time that had forced itself between us, irresistible, made up of the unfixed, changeable material of language and innumerable other mutabilities: it no longer exists. All thick centuries-old walls dissolve in the face of a naked, unhappy person.

I read the passage in his diary again. Why he so senselessly and so unconditionally wanted this war – to defeat *English mercantilism*, to let the German *bell of renewal* ring out – does he at this hour himself still know what the reason was?

When he wakes up, he beholds the swineherd. He puts him up against – no, *before* his son. Now, in the middle of the war, a new time begins, a renewal that will happen not to the German people but to him alone. For he doesn't only have these two dead men on his conscience, the swineherd and the son. The war, this murdering carnage, that's something he wanted, that's true, but more than that, he needed it. He needed it the way a volcano needs to erupt, the way stormy sultriness needs lightning and thunder: as the unavoidable discharge of an extreme inner tension, as the shattering of a tangled knotting in chest and head, as the uncramping of his intellectual musculature.

Behind the swineherd and the son millions of dead line up, untold numbers of wounded and maimed. In endless columns they walk past him day and night, or sit on street corners, their empty trouser legs or sleeves carefully tied up, a cap in their lap in whose hollows lie a few small coins.

He has all of them on his conscience.

Of course that's not true. How can one individual bear so much responsibility?

And yet it *is* true. His hurrays, and the hurrays of the others, still ring in his ears. Within a few months he's become quiet and subdued. More quiet and subdued than he's ever been. His conscience knows what it's responsible for. He trusts it. And he notices that along with this, he once again has faith in God. For he's unable to think of his conscience and his faith separated from one another. He doesn't even try to. For the first time since leaving his parish in Połajewo, he receives the sacrament again.

Conscience: what a strange, beautiful thing it is! In our conscience lies the felt knowledge of right and wrong. But where does it come from? Who gave it to us? Is it one of the many mutabilities that distinguish us from those who lived before us? Is it connected to God as insolubly as Sanderling feels it to be? Why do we even still have a conscience? For we do still have one, even if we don't often listen to it.

Perhaps this is how it is: the direction conscience turns us towards, what it burdens us with, is changeable. Not just from era to era; from person to person it changes its voice. But that such a voice exists, this strange entity planted deep inside us, not to be banished or else to be driven deeper inside us, this confidant that knows about and judges all our deeds, even the ones known only to us, even the ones we ourselves don't even know about yet, and all our thoughts, hasn't that been the case ever since human beings have been able to give witness about themselves and their inner struggles? Thus conscience abolishes time. There's no time separating me from someone who ungags this stranger in themselves and allows it to speak. Such a person is my fellow human being, however far away from me they may be: the stranger living inside them is more familiar to me than they themselves are; they're our shared friend and foe. This friend-foe is not one to be satisfied with ideas. They want to see deeds. But which ones?

In something Sanderling published later, the word *perpetrator* jumps out at me. But how far away it is from its current exclusive meaning! It's hard to believe, but for

Sanderling perpetrators are the opposite of thinkers. It's as if I'm seeing the word for the first time in its infancy, never to be brought back. Almost with tenderness, I observe how it inserts itself into the sentence in which it occupies the nice role of the craftsman. Ten years later, it's already well on the way to its new counterpart, the victim.

But let us return once more to the Great War.

In 1914, Sanderling still had ten years to live, but only I know that. I'd like to pester him, would like to shout at him: You don't have all the time in the world! You've already taken lots of detours and wrong tracks, you've thrown yourself with beautiful or staggering absoluteness into this or that task. Now pull yourself together, turn your attention to what really matters. And try to bring it to a conclusion.

Sanderling isn't about to accept any advice from his distant descendant. He lives on – doesn't simply live out his life, no, that's not something he ever did. He's one of those people who never gets tired. Instead, he bestirs himself more than ever in all directions at once, the actual and practical as well as the intellectual. Where does the path between those two run, he asks himself time and again. But time and again, in his groping search, he ends up too far away from all plausible paths and from the middle way he's so passionately and laboriously seeking, including in his life's final great efforts.

In 1917 he's appointed the second director of the Raiffeisen cooperative in Berlin. Originally, a Raiffeisen cooperative bank was an organization made up of at least seven farmers who sought to protect themselves together against exploitative moneylenders. This evolved into both powerful local associations and financial institutions operating worldwide which represent the same interests as any other bank. Friedrich Wilhelm Raiffeisen was a devout Christian who was convinced that such associations could not serve self-interest and might only subsist 'if they're founded on the basis of unconditional self-help, that is, are only made up of people who personally require aid'. By 1917, Raiffeisen had been dead for nearly thirty years.

Rather than people working towards the common good, what Sanderling observes is many of them pursuing 'united self-interest'. He only remains in the position for three years. However much he feels driven towards practical engagement, he seldom lasts longer than a few years in a single activity. The harder he tries, the more he sees the two poles, 'real' and 'ideal', pull away from each other. Yet for him those two poles aren't distant airy forms but the two ends of the rack he's tied down to, his own painful extremities.

In Berlin he meets up with Gutkind and Buber again. These two reinforce, *if that was still necessary*, his oppressive feeling *that this war could never have broken out and been conducted as it has been, if we Potsdam men had been what we wanted to be – an intellectually solid class of inner authority against the world's helpless anxiety.*

By *we Potsdam men* he means those eight who met up shortly before the war, that *pneumatic society* which in its only ever meeting began to unhinge the world; the so-called Forte Circle, which bore power in its name but never got far beyond that name. Today, nearly all these people have been forgotten.

It's not only the shame over having cheered along and participated. It's also not only the awareness of having the swineherd and his own son on his conscience. Sanderling is convinced that he, with a handful of others, could have prevented the war. Hard to believe. Who is this man, that he believes he could steer the fate of the country, no, of Europe and the world? How does he arrive at the unshakeable conviction – perhaps the only one of his convictions that doesn't seem to have been subject to constant convulsions – of his own significance, the importance of his own decisions and actions for the continuation of history? You aren't Napoleon, I'd like to shout at him, nor are you Bismarck or Alexander the Great.

In the small pre-war circle of men with delusions of grandeur he is perhaps the one with the most extreme delusions of grandeur.

Where does this self-confidence come from? Does it have some foundation, or is it hubris? Does he draw it from his own certainly not negligible intellectual powers? Does it run in the family? Is it both?

I have to think about the way the pastor Sanderling, in Połajewo, wanted to himself teach his eldest son, the one who was later killed in the war, and in doing so felt burdened by the weight of all of humanity and godliness. By now he's not been a cleric for some time, but the weight has continued to burden his soul.

His delusions of grandeur express themselves less in sensual feelings of power than in immoderate, long-lasting pangs of conscience. He realizes he had substituted for the lost kingdom of God a German empire that in his eyes could only be Prussian. For him, God's place had been taken by Old Fritz (Frederick the Great). And indeed: at our virtually intergalactic distance from our forefathers, the two of them do share a certain similarity.

To be sure, it's hard not to sneer. Nothing is easier: even a small distance makes what others once took terribly seriously seem laughable and absurd. I only need to give in to this impulse. As punishment, the same will happen to me. No, I'm not going to run even that risk: the seriousness, *that* seriousness, hasn't survived, over the course of the century it has, along with everything else, perished. The ironizers ambush with their arrows from a safe place. But is it something to be laughed at if someone believes in a state as if in a new divinity? Others whom we don't smile about and whom we still honour today have with no less bloody consequences exchanged the rule of God for that of the proletariat. I resist the temptation to disguise my dread beneath scorn.

Sanderling didn't forget the words with which, shortly after the start of the war, he informed his *dear friends of the circle* that he would not be attending the planned second meeting: he told them he was now *nothing but blood and nerves, nothing but a trembling warhorse*. Not only *the warhorse of the German army, but a part of the angel who bears eternity.*

The trembling warhorse never fought in any war. He was past the age to serve as a soldier. So he did what he was suited to do: he sat and devoted himself to administrative tasks. And that's where he trembled. As a part of the angel who bears eternity?

Sanderling had a feeling for many things, but not for his own ridiculousness. Would it perhaps be a possible salvation, I think, if nobody ever lacked that feeling? Then nobody would give themselves airs, nobody would carry out imperious gestures and quake like warhorses. Yet I try in vain to clearly distinguish between beautiful enthusiasm, stormy, passionate liveliness and fanaticism, hysteria and finally stupidity. So how might we banish the latter from the world and preserve the former? And if a heightened sense of your own ridiculousness prevailed, would violent acts still happen at all? Further: by what means might you develop that sense? Should every German school pupil – perhaps it would be somewhat less urgent with the others – have two hours of lessons per week on ridiculousness studies?

My gaze returns to Sanderling's warhorse. How briefly it gallops away, how soon it stumbles! Who could make fun of someone who's lying on the ground, feeling ashamed of himself and his bloodthirsty rapture, which he now recognizes as *drunkenness*. The intoxication has passed. The time of carnival is over.

I again pick up his book on the origins of carnival: humanity transforms into *cannibalistic bloodthirstiness*; during the Festival of Dionysus, the royal mother rips her son to pieces while he's still alive, and the society ladies fall upon him *like hunting dogs in a cattle enclosure*. The *gobbling of raw flesh* is part of the cult due to this god.

In the course of four years, seventeen million people were gobbled up. To even come close to reaching such a number, I need several large cities, and even wishing to keep track of a single such city is hopeless; I think of the swarm of people in Paris and its surroundings, which supposedly amount to around twelve million. Dionysus overate. He was stricken with severe indigestion. You might think he wouldn't be able to swallow even one bite more for centuries. Anyone born a few decades later doesn't believe it. They know: the greed of this god is unlimited.

For the Babylonians, Sanderling writes, the earth was an image of heaven. They brought all earthly events into harmony with the laws of heaven, with the paths of the heavenly bodies. They saw the stars as signs of life, revelations by the gods – and *now we can imagine the scale of the earthquake that struck Chaldea when the calculation didn't in the end add up, when the harmony between heaven and earth ruptured, when the two greatest revelatory gods, Sun and Moon, couldn't be reconciled!*

So that the calculation did work out, those who came afterwards inserted an extra day every four years. But anxiety and terror were in the world. It was over the notion that at certain times *moon and sun fail in their service to heaven at the same time* that the rhythm of moon and sun are not in perfect harmony, that the *calendar-hole of disorder* opened up, that the rage of carnival broke out. Reason veered into unreason, humanity into scorn for humanity. The short interregnum of *Prince Carnival* began. Yet perhaps, writes Sanderling, this stuttering of time, this disturbance of its beautiful regularity, did not first and foremost generate anxiety at all but on the contrary corresponded with a deep human need for unleashing, intoxication and bestiality.

I don't know how it was among the Babylonians, have enough trouble imagining myself back by a century; how much further am I from the Babylonians, from whose point of view Sanderling and I are more or less contemporaries. But I do have some conception of Kleist and Cervantes, and so I have the not undeceptive but nonetheless very certain feeling that in his essay about carnival he was speaking just as little about the Babylonians as earlier he was about Kleist or Cervantes. In 1909 he presents his ideas on the origins of carnival in a nearly two-hour lecture to the Vienna Sociological Society, where his listeners included Hofmannsthal, who naturally reached a different judgement from mine, though am I judging? No, I feel more than I think: what he's revealing here is his own inner frenzy, his own longing to be unleashed and wild, which he's always controlled with decisiveness and force of will. It's his own insanity; the same as he saw reflected, years earlier, in the raging Hercules of the asylum in Poznań.

Now he's endowing the Babylonians with it! And he's doing so five years before war broke out. The modern man he writes about is himself, who, seen from today, is as unmodern as possible. *An earthquake goes through his chest when the voices of the frenzy threaten his work, when there's a war in sight, when an outcry of suppressed cravings bays against the discipline he's inflicted upon himself.* Is it possible you are never the only one to think or feel in one way or another? That what we take to be our individual sensibility is never more than the reflection of a collective sensibility? Or at least to a considerable extent?

It's not merely his own insanity that rumbles in him. For him, medieval carnival isn't worth talking about. Now is the moment, it's now that the time fallen out of time has come again, in his own, German present. Like a Native American he puts his ear to the ground and with anxiety and desire perceives the quaking of the old, barbaric carnival. The one short day is approaching on which enslaved people will be masters and the gods will be scorned. The day of the great murderous carnage. The day when time stands still. By the evening of this day he will have torn his own son to shreds with his teeth. He doesn't recognize the trembling warhorse in the mirror. It's the hour of sobriety.

In Normandy, it's late August; the warmest days of summer have already passed. Not far from the coast, I sit outside at night, tilting my head back and letting the shooting stars fall into my eyes. Behind the stars that shine up above me there are always new, invisible stars moving along their orbits, at some point no longer reachable with any telescope. These constellations, which disappear into unimaginable expanses, conform to a certain regularity. This regularity isn't absolute, though; it encompasses slight variations. Is it really the case that something leads from these slight variations to frenzy and carnage? I'm trying to follow Sanderling's train of thought, I want to take him as seriously as he took himself, I'm honestly exerting myself to do so. He doesn't seem to have struck either Hofmannsthal or Benjamin, who both knew his writings, as questionable; on the contrary. Why do his ideas not make sense to me? I'm standing alone before these three great intellects and I fumble around with the toy weapons of my mind. Isn't our solar calendar a vain attempt to get the unthinkable breadth and depth of heaven down on graph paper? To turn the orbits of the stars into the timetable of the Deutsche Bahn? The calendar is an approximation. What's revealed by the calendar is the impossibility of bringing heavenly time into agreement with human time. That's how it seems to me as the stars swim in my wide-open eyes as if in the nearby sea.

Why should that insight have led to derisive laughter towards the gods and finally, because they're too far away, a universal slaughter? Are reason and unreason, order and disorder, a matter for the gods? Is the world supposed to have collapsed for the Babylonians because the stars refused to march in formation like a Prussian infantry regiment? I draw my wooden sword and say right into the faces of the three great ones: This is where the carnage, the lust for gruesomeness, the urge to break free of all obligations, get placed beneath celestial vaults. For what would remain of them without that overpowering dome?

Next morning I'm leafing through a special issue of the newspaper *La Manche Libre* marking the anniversary of its founding in 1944, shortly after the liberation of the département. I look at the photographs of towns near where I'm currently sitting. Saint-Lô, Avranches, Caen, Coutances, Valognes all lie in ruins. The only Germans you see are either dead or have their hands up. I pause at a sunny street scene full of people who are all walking towards the camera but without looking forwards; instead they look at two women in the centre. Beneath their shaven heads the women have their faces turned down. In the crowd of people driving them through the town you can hardly see any women; it's men and boys who on foot or on bicycles accompany the two women and have their heads turned towards them, some laughing, others shouting something at them – the sound was turned down long ago, so much the better. A lanky boy with glasses, wearing shorts and a short-sleeved shirt buttoned up to the collar and long socks, walks right next to the bigger of the two women; he's smiling lewdly and making an obscene gesture. The gaping mouths, the nasty, scornful looks all directed at the two denounced women, their downward-turned gazes, the structure of the picture highlighting the suffering remind me of the old painted depictions of the way of the Cross. The taunters, the henchmen, the torturers, there they go. But where is the weeping mother, the powerless, inconsolable friend?

A caption under the photograph explains how many women in the La Manche département alone were led through the streets with shaven heads. They were accused of so-called 'horizontal collaboration', that is, of having sexual relationships with Germans, but it sufficed that they had done business with them or even merely lived in the same building. I read that on 14 July 1944 in Cherbourg, a dozen women, having first had their heads shaved in public, had to climb into a trailer on which they were driven through the streets of the town accompanied by drum rolls. This vehicle was called the '*Char des collaboratrices*'. These processions, which took place in almost the entire country, are known by the name '*carnaval moche*': ugly carnival. That year, 1944, was a leap year.

I also learn from the caption that to prevent further spontaneous punishments of this kind, France's transitional government passed laws about suspected collaboration with the enemy. The desire to torment and humiliate was to be placed in a legal framework. I read that among other kinds of collaboration, punishments were laid out for '*collaboration sentimentale*' or '*amicale*'. Love for the enemy.

The enemy of the French is always the Germans, and that of the Germans is always the French. That leads me back to Sanderling and to his last book, *Deutsche Bauhütte*, published in 1924, which I still haven't read because I haven't been able to charm it out of either my father or the archive in Berlin, not even as a photocopy, though I do know that in it he urges the Germans to participate first-hand in the reconstruction of France and

Belgium. The book can hardly be found anywhere; it seems to have been published in a very small print run. All of two copies are to be found for sale on the internet, for a high price. I finally bring myself to order the least expensive of the two (with markings) from an antiquarian bookstore in Lübeck.

While I'm waiting for the book I ordered, I mull over Benjamin's historical theses, which do have something to do with Sanderling's theories about carnival. It was through the Gutkinds that Sanderling befriended Benjamin, who intended to publish his essay on carnival in the first issue of *Angelus Novus*, the journal Benjamin planned but which never appeared.

Benjamin's carnival doesn't take long to get called revolution. Time standing still is brought about not by movements in the sky but among people. In various places in Paris during the July Revolution, he writes, on the evening of the first day of conflict, people shot at clocks in towers. The old time was supposed to come to a halt, a new time to begin. The time in between, the instant outside time when reversal sets in, belongs to the unleashed, the extraordinary, the lawless. Except that the teeth-baring of this carnival is aimed not at the gods but at the rulers. I read the clumsy alexandrines of the immortal Joseph Méry which illustrate this thesis, the fifteenth. It seems to me about as sensible to shoot at a clock as it would at a thermometer if you're finding it too cold or too hot. At the same time I feel as if I've taken up the Talmud and now have the presumptuousness to try and understand it. The theses on history don't take up more than a few pages. The quintessence of the incomprehensible. It's said. And yet I do understand something here and there. No sooner do I have the feeling I've understood something than I become suspicious. That can't be right! I start over again from the beginning. And so it goes on. With the seventh thesis, I have the impression that it applies to me personally. My mistrust towards this impression is of course limitless, but I can't ward it off entirely. What brings me to this presumptuous thought is the word *empathy*, which I'm probably understanding incorrectly, namely as a movement of the soul. What's meant instead of that, I can only guess: a taking-over of the point of view? Aligning yourself with the prevailing conditions? In the seventh thesis, which provokes extreme contradiction in me, two possibilities for observing history are juxtaposed: historicism and historical materialism. The first approach, customary in the nineteenth century, was, Benjamin writes, about empathy. 'Its origin lies in the indolence of the heart, the acedia that despairs of mastering the true historical picture that fleetingly shines.' I don't grasp how empathy can be based on indolence of the heart – isn't empathy on the contrary the most extreme exertion of the heart? This indolence of the heart or deep sadness comes, he argues, from the fact that the writer of history is always empathizing with the rulers and victors. The same was true of Flaubert when he wrote *Salammbô*.

Is that correct? I dare to ask myself. I reread *Salammbô*. What triumphs there is indeed Carthage, but not as an oppressive regime; instead it is an empire of wild, riotous sensuality. The novel takes place shortly after the First Punic War and narrates the love of the mercenary Mathô, a Barbarian, for Hamilcar's daughter. In the end, Mathô dies an unimaginably gruesome death before Salammbô's eyes, a death by torture dedicated to her. Mathô, the loving mercenary who dies for his love, is juxtaposed with the ruler Hamilcar, a cold-blooded, unscrupulous military strategist who ends up having his own daughter poisoned. It strikes me as unlikely that Flaubert sides with Hamilcar.

It seems to me, moreover, that there's an error in Benjamin's reasoning (presumably next I'll be proving to Einstein that he committed a minor mistake in his theory). The process of empathy is supposed to have its origin in the indolence of the heart or in sadness. At the same time, sadness only arises as a result of empathy in that it is always identification with the rulers. But how can indolence of the heart or sadness be the origin and result of one and the same phenomenon – empathy?

I call my friend Pierre, the man with the Easter Island head and one of the cleverest people I know – in his case it's not only the Moai head but also the heart and all the senses that do the thinking – and ask him to explain Benjamin's seventh thesis on history to me. In no time at all he has pulled the French translation of the book from his shelves.

We agree that Flaubert isn't on the side of the victors. Why should a writer who takes on historical material inevitably identify with the victors? Isn't a writer on the contrary a person for whom any empathy for the victors, unless they ultimately are unmasked as losers, is alien?

I ask Pierre how Benjamin could have distanced himself so far from his own free ways of thinking and got diverted into the paths of a pre-existing view of the world and of history. '*Bon, bon, ne m'engueule pas!*' says Pierre: fine, don't shout at me. As always happens when something provokes my spirit of contradiction and I start to get worked up, Pierre enjoys himself by pretending to think my indignation is aimed at him.

Besides, I say, I don't understand why identifying with the winners, if you manage to do so, should make you sad. The winners are very pleased with themselves, marching forwards in the best possible mood on their unscrupulous triumphal procession. So why should those who recognize themselves in them be unhappy?

Because they have a guilty conscience, says Pierre. It doesn't actually say that, but the idea could be that those who put themselves in the place of the rulers have a guilty conscience towards the losers they have neglected. That they feel an indistinct, muffled pain.

That partly explains things to me, even if I don't understand why only those who sympathize with them, and not the victors themselves, should feel this pain. Wouldn't they have more reason to do so?

I ask Pierre what the true historical picture looks like, the one Benjamin writes about that fleetingly shines. The image that can only be recognized by those who haven't succumbed to that empathizing sadness and indolence of the heart.

Benjamin was desperate, says Pierre. In his desperation, he convinced himself and others that he believed in historical materialism. In salvation, in the fulfilment of all hopes.

Pierre has now warmed up; his voice follows the abrupt accelerations of his thoughts. For a long time, he tells me, it remained unclear to him how to make sense of Benjamin's messianism, until a few years ago a black taxi driver in Lisbon who had spent a lot of time thinking passionately about this question made it somewhat comprehensible to him. Driven into a corner, without any hope for the future, Benjamin displaced the moment of salvation into the present. For the person whose heart wasn't too lazy to detect it, that image of salvation flashes at once like lightning. Benjamin knew that no better times lay ahead. And yet the present hides their possibility: a sparse series of possibilities that are never realized.

I owe it to an unknown taxi driver in Lisbon that I now also believe I've understood something (*méfiance, méfiance*): what Benjamin perhaps meant by this 'true historical picture' was this sliver of hope hidden in the present.

Anything is permitted to someone without hope, I think. Even believing in historical materialism as if in a new Messiah.

The theses on history are among the last sentences Benjamin wrote down. The next morning, Sanderling's last printed words are lying in my letterbox: the book *Deutsche Bauhütte*, which appeared in 1924. Neither Benjamin's theses nor this *Bauhütte* were meant to be testaments; a quick death made them that. I look at the faded red on the upper edge of the paperback cover. The title is printed in broken letters, subtitle and author's name in a rounded typography that resembles today's fonts; thus the book promises both: new and old.

Already in the book's opening words, what appears is an individual speaking to a large number of other individuals. The sound of this voice touches me in a wonderful way. I thought I already knew it. And indeed, the old hardness, the old fire, are still there, but burned down to a brightly smouldering glow. A cramped quality has loosened. Until now, anything simple was an impossibility, and no doubt that is still the case. But the reader is no longer suffocated by tortuous convolutions of words. I breathe freely through the opening pages, astonished about the person I encounter, one I had never seen before. *You don't so much write such things as you are written by them.* That's it. I wouldn't have been able to put it into words so quickly, but that's it: the man standing before me is a written person. Some essays or testimonies, the fruit of long and intense struggles and transformations of the soul, reach us, like this one, more alive than dead.

I'm spellbound as I read on. It was to think these thoughts that Sanderling set out a long time earlier. Without restraint or hesitation, he threw himself into things in many different directions, devoted himself first to Christianity then to Prussianness, without ever managing his resources. I've accompanied him on the brusque back and forth of his meanderings, have climbed down at his side into the abyss. I only had one advantage over him: time. I knew how things would develop after his death.

And contrary to my resolve not to look, I did involuntarily search for signs that what was to come might have been hinted at, so I could move forward and back from one vanished generation to the next as if on the strung-together boards of a rotting hanging bridge. I thought I had found such a portent in Sanderling's visit to the asylum. But the generations of a family aren't well suited to building a bridge. In contrast to what I had thought and feared, I didn't penetrate to *the*, not even to *an* origin of the Made-in-Germany murders. No, that cannot be found in Sanderling. The path breaks off. The path indicated by his final work would not have led over corpses. Sanderling stood at the fork in the road and shouted with a clear voice. But nobody heard him.

Now that his life is coming to an end, I see him on a high place that looks out in all directions, and I notice how he generously and powerfully pulls me up to him. I didn't know it when I began the journey, but it's clear to me now: I set out back then in order to think through these ideas.

'*Cet homme est fou!*' Yes, he's crazy, and more than ever, but in a new, beautiful way. Sanderling is now struggling, with the same absoluteness he's brought to everything else, to find a middle ground. The middle way he's seeking is more than ever that *between real and ideal*, between hands-on action and an unattainable goal. If a crusader or ayatollah suddenly set out to preach reason and moderation everywhere, it couldn't seem more peculiar. But is what he's promoting moderate and reasonable? The war has been lost; the misery all around is just as great as the indignation about the treaty demanded by the victors. Doesn't what Sanderling considers the middle lie as always much nearer to the *ideal* than the *real*?

His book's most important practical demand is one that must strike everyone besides him as futile: here we have an individual German addressing all other individual Germans and imploring them to take an active part in helping with the reconstruction of the areas of France and Belgium that were destroyed by them during the war. To make repairs, not just beyond the damages demanded by the victors and conceded by Germany; no: completely independent of those.

Without question, the situation is one that makes his appeal especially hopeless, but would it have been less so in a different situation? Has it happened even once in human history that after a war the defeated have rebuilt the houses of the victors? Or even the victors the houses of the defeated? That anyone at all has been concerned with anything other than their own spared life, their own house and belongings? '*Cet homme est fou.*'

The middle way he's pointing to is in reality a high mountain path. No trees grow up there; the air gets thinner and thinner. He doesn't notice, he forges ahead. For the first time in his life he thinks he's discovered a desirable middle way. Come! he confidently shouts to the others. And doesn't see that he's walking totally alone on a ridge up above ravines of ice.

It's hard not to think at this point of the illness from which he is soon to die. Of course, life is not cause and illness is not effect, any more than one era leads directly to the next. And yet: can it be a coincidence that Sanderling's illness begins in the spine? Is the backbone not the firm, invisible centre of the body? Isn't the whole body suspended on the column of the vertebrae? The spinal cord is the most internal middle of a human being. Part of the *central* nervous system.

But the illness in the centre has not yet broken out. From up on the mountain path that he considers passable, Sanderling turns to his fellow countrymen, not as a different, better, cleverer person, but as one of them; he speaks not only to them but also to himself, urges the majority of the individuals not to keep failing to hear or to drown out the voice of their conscience. For their conscience tells them, must tell them, that they are hiding behind a generality, behind their representatives, who want to cleverly lie their way out of responsibility. It tells them that they themselves, each one independently, must stand up and help their neighbours. It doesn't care what others have been responsible for, doesn't recognize the scales they might use to play down their own misdeeds. Conscience knows only one pressing onus, the inner command which shall not be pushed away. The 'ambiguity of inner warning'.

Few people can ever have stood so alone as Sanderling at this point. The few short written contributions printed at the back of the book, partly in agreement, partly in scepticism, by Benjamin, Buber and a few others, only make him seem even more alone. Fearlessly and decisively, he steps forward before a desperate, hungry, furious crowd to bring them to their senses.

No, that's nonsense. He doesn't step in front of any crowd of people. He addresses all Germans, yes, but not as a mass. Masses, nations, he writes, have no conscience. He addresses individuals who should not come together but remain as single as they are, at most forming manageably small cells. And they should offer help to other individuals, their neighbours.

He doesn't make accusations. He suffers pangs of conscience, speaks from deepest distress – for himself and as the representative of the others. Didn't they, like him, want war? Didn't they sacrifice their sons to a false god? Didn't they believe the lies told by those for whom the war was a gigantic game of chess? Those who played for all or nothing and lost? (Only the game, not their lives.)

I read, not in Sanderling's book but in a historical text, Ludendorff's answer to the question of what would happen if the last great offensive should fail: 'Then Germany would be destroyed.' Almost the exact same sentence will be heard again on different lips towards the end of the next war. Sanderling won't be around to hear it. Besides which, he's not interested in the big players. He isn't making accusations, even of those who are clearly guilty. The powerful men, the generals and statesmen of all nations, he doesn't honour them with a single word. He's indifferent to which country at which point in the war was responsible for this or that thing. Conscience demands silence from the kind of thinking that weighs things up.

There's a peculiar thing about reading a book. For the most part, the reader glides over the surface of the words, only able or wishing to move forwards, not to dive into the depths. Yet there are books or particular passages that make it hard for the reader to flee, that grab them. This is one of those books. I read the pages in which Sanderling speaks of conscience, and feel how much I'm gripped, seized. And in doing so I witness a remarkable transformation: this man who expressed himself with pathos about subjects for which I could barely summon up a tinge of warmth, and whose strictness and absoluteness so often made me cringe, how differently he speaks here! For decades he struggled and sought, continually throwing himself at new goals only to turn back around full of anger and disappointment; with his lack of calm and moderation, he bestowed upon himself and those closest to him a hard, uncomfortable life. Shaking my head, I observed him, and frequently – as respectfully as possible – I smiled at him. And now?

Now there stands before me an unknown man who fills me with reverence.

Wisdom isn't quite what he achieves at the end of his life; or is wisdom crazy? What is it then? It's greatness, and it's beauty. His book has the beauty of a person who doesn't realize how beautiful he is. Who never strove for beauty. What did he strive for? For something that he himself would not have been able to name. Beauty came about incidentally. Beauty is the congruence in one person of both extreme distress and the highest development of his possibilities and his word.

In the beginning, there is overwhelmed looking, being astonished, keeping quiet, when the 'craving to take hold of, to rule, to subordinate' is turned off and the human being 'simply takes in', 'obeying the revelation that is presented to him'. That's how looking operates for Plato, for Goethe – and for Sanderling, who quotes them and adds: *an idea that imposes itself is also a revelation, and wishes, like any other phenomenon, to be taken in in an overwhelmed state.* He includes among those ideas the demands of conscience.

Obviously he's concerned with the here and now, with Germany's situation after the Great War. The demand of conscience he refers to is the one of the moment; it wants the reconstruction of the devastated neighbouring countries. But he's also and perhaps more concerned with every coming here and now. With a *lasting opposition to the prevailing circumstances*, a *lasting unsettling of conscience*, that *unsettles the state by virtue of the fact the citizens' conscience shames and completes it, incalculably, also fitfully, but not in a single jerk.* This lasting unsettling of conscience, he writes, is the real not yet fulfilled German revolution. The previous revolutions were, for him, class revolutions, *against* something, against the individual, against the ruler, the oppressor, yet they got stuck in class conflict and never attained *human universality*. He says: *The continuation of the revolution will no longer happen on the level of class; it's transferred over to the individual*. It must be a revolution for the individual.

That's a big idea, one I'm now taking in with amazement; overwhelmed, I think it over and through and feel it. Yes, the wheel of conscience is one that keeps on turning. It never stands still, never rests, is never satisfied with itself and the world. In contrast to every other revolution, this one doesn't work towards its own end. Its goal is never reached. Conscience can never be turned off.

At this point in the book, I stumble on a most curious image: an idea, Sanderling writes, is *a being in itself that couldn't be foreseen* which *appears suddenly like a child barging in on the parental couple. That goes* its own *way, has its own shape and figure*, its own *needs and capabilities.*' What our conscience demands of us is *an idea that forces a duty into our soul*.

Further on, he takes up this image again slightly differently, and in a way I find strangely moving: the demand on conscience is scorned *by the recognized intellectual giants* as an *illegitimate child*. The German revolution that, as he writes, the world is still waiting for, the political philosophy that his book develops – they rest, to my secret joy, on that extramarital, despised child of conscience who must survive outside of any established order and make its own way. This strange image is of course not what I want to see in it: a wave of the hand aimed at me across the years and the generations. Unless such a wave might originate just as much in the person who receives it as in the one who makes it?

Now that I've almost finished reading the book, I'm struck by an odd concurrence: in 1924, for Sanderling, all people should succumb to their longing for *human communality, for unifying action*, the voices of all should harmonize, whether Catholic, Protestant, Jewish or devoid of all religion; this one man calls for people not to relinquish their own personal responsibility for what happens in their country to any authority or any representative of the people, and wishes to stretch out a helping hand to the neighbours; at the same time, another man is, from a prison in Landsberg, calling for hatred. All blame and responsibility should be placed upon those who are hated. Even without owning the soon-to-be published Braille edition, a blind person can understand the Book of Hate. The printed copies number in the millions. The *Deutsche Bauhütte* will sink to the bottom.

At last I believe I've understood what the Deutschtum was that Benjamin saw embodied in Sanderling. What it could have been. And I bow down before the crazy man with the reddish hair who lent it a human figure even though he himself knew best of all how imperfect that figure was. And how imperfect his book must therefore also be: *It couldn't have been any other way than that the word grew darker on the way from the origin to the conclusion; its simplicity dimmed in the multiplicity of the idea, the pure thing in what was never overcome in the person of the author.*

I bow down before someone who for his whole life tried to overcome the human being inside him and in the end developed some affection for that human being. And I recognize that that very thing – the human being – was the middle way towards which in his later years he was striving.

Shortly after closing the book, I leave for Poland. In that old, ill-defined middle: Central Europe. What do I expect to learn there more than a century on? I'm travelling to Poznań, 123 years after Sanderling settled there.

It begins – once more, one last time in this chronicle of a journey through time, something begins – with my failure to find the exit from the railway station in Poznań. I wander up and down the platform, carrying my suitcase back and forth; there's no sign of a way to get out, and the track where my train came in is crammed between other tracks and seems not to be connected to the outside world. Yet the other people who got off the train must have disappeared somewhere! I end up asking a young woman how to find the exit. She looks around and first has to think it over, as if she herself had just been conjured up onto this platform. Then it occurs to her that over there somewhere, right in the back, at the end of the platform, there must be a way out. And indeed, I drag my suitcase up one flight of stairs then down another and up another and finally find myself standing by a highway.

The suitcase with its hard plastic wheels rumbles over the paving stones (not cobblestones), though the sound is drowned out by the noise of the cars. A monumental glass bulge comes into view right near me, a kind of airship hangar in which a gigantic Zeppelin would have plenty of room. I slowly realize that it must be the station I've finally escaped, but I can't associate the glittering form with the dismal platform I walked up and down.

It's already dark. The streets get narrower and lead uphill and downhill; into the heart of the past, perhaps. Into a fabricated past reconstructed stone by stone in fresh pastel colours. Everything made unhappened, unseen. The old town is a stage set where presumably in the summer tourists sit drinking coffee and beer. Now it's nearly November.

At nine o'clock on the evening I arrive, I stand in front of the town hall looking around as I wait for Anna, whom I've arranged to meet. We've never seen each other before. The few people who pause in front of the dark building don't look over towards me. Will she come? After a while, my phone buzzes. It's Anna, who's been standing three steps away the whole time and was looking in another direction. Out of shyness? Out of mischief, I'm more inclined to believe.

Right away she's close to me, yet we're not in the least bit close. Friendship, or love, is decided in a few moments by virtually wordless processes, like hands touching in greeting or expressions in the corner of an eye. Can it be? Five minutes after we've recognized each other, two hours after my arrival in the city, I'm friends with a Polish woman.

My Polish is limited to *dzień dobry* and *do widzenia*, but years ago Anna was an au pair for a family of Green politicians in Hanover and speaks German well. I tell her about Sanderling (whom I don't call Sanderling), and about the questions I'm asking myself. About Germany and Poland, about the past, how it was and is. Anna is friendly; no, more than friendly. Agnieszka in Paris, through whom I got to know Anna, Slawomir, Agata and Karolina, whom I'll later meet up with in Poznań: none of the Poles I meet seems to have anything against Germans. Yet the past throbs in everything they tell me. And through their words and faces, the Germans confront me as hardheaded, terror-inducing, dark figures. The Germans? In their words and faces I encounter myself.

The second time we meet up, a few days later, Anna tells me the good news of the day is that the trains no longer run on time in Germany either. This was reported in the news that morning. She laughs and I laugh too; why not, it's funny. The Germans are upset that their train system is no longer what it once was. For everyone else this is good news. I have to think about the testimony I read in Raul Hilberg. Later I spend a long time looking for it and finally find it on page 622 of the second volume. It comes from a former internee of the Dutch camp Westerbork: 'The train keeps precisely to its timetable, and this is a horror and a torture. It never runs late, it's never hit by a bomb.'

Later I will get to know Anna's husband, Marek, who doesn't speak any German. I say to him everything I can say in Polish: *dzień dobry, do widzenia, dziękuję*. He responds with all the German words he knows: *Hände hoch! Nicht schießen! Verfluchte polnische Schweine!* A German–Polish conversation.

I'm glad I don't stand out to anyone in Poznań as a German. In truth I'm always glad not to stand out as a German, and I find it hard to imagine Germans who feel differently, though I'm sure there are some. I do well at keeping a low profile in Poznań: in the street, several times, people ask me for directions. I add *nie mówię po polsku* to my vocabulary.

It's a big city. But through a coincidence I don't consider a coincidence, right near my hotel – I only need to walk to the end of the small street – is the former synagogue. Cécile had already told me in Paris that the Poznań synagogue had been turned into a public swimming pool. On my first night there I discover from a street plan that I'm practically sleeping next door.

I go there the next morning. If I hadn't known its location, I don't think I'd have taken the building for either a synagogue or a swimming pool. From the side it looks like a run-down block of flats, with regular rows of small windows, and damp has sketched cloudy forms in the plaster. The front facade doesn't look like anything in particular. Some kind of exhibition hall, perhaps? Above the big glass facade a large poster hangs, on which I recognize, among many other names, Bill Viola and Nick Cave. Some kind of art festival? The building is locked and dilapidated.

Later I buy a book which reproduces exterior and interior views of the synagogue from the past and today. The foundation stone was laid in 1906, two years after Sanderling left Poznań. The old photo shows a splendid building with domes, towers and all manner of decorations on gables and windows. The present-day building looks as if it was constructed in the 1960s. The old outlines can be vaguely discerned, but all the roundedness and ornamentation, all the towers and domes have disappeared. It's as if Cologne's cathedral had been rebuilt as a tall, elongated hangar with a flat roof and with anything Gothic or otherwise striking hewn off.

I remember we laughed, Cécile and I, when she told me about the synagogue converted into a swimming pool; it seemed on the outside like laughter, but in reality it was the expression of our bewilderment and speechlessness.

In the colour photographs of the synagogue before it was partially destroyed I observe the painted stucco decorations of the domes, the women's galleries on either side, and in a niche at the head of the room I think I can make out the shrine, the Holy Ark where the Torah scrolls are kept.

The photo from 2012 shows the same room now with blue-green tiles, the vaults easily recognizable. The women's galleries have now become changing rooms, the prayer room is where the – empty – swimming pool is situated.

I gather from the accompanying text that the conversion of the synagogue into a swimming pool began in April 1940 and that after the war the Poles continued to use it as a pool, up until only a few years ago, in this century, when Poland's Jewish community had their house of worship restored to them in the form of a thoroughly rundown swimming pool. It was supposed to be turned into a centre for dialogue and tolerance. 'But for the time being, due to inadequate funding, the project has been put on ice.' First water. Then ice. Desecration is even worse than destruction. I don't know why this picture in particular has such an effect on me, but the swimming pool is, after all the many things I've read and looked at in the last several months, the drop, thousands of litres in size, that makes what has been blocked up inside me spill over. Is it the high-handed cold of those tiles in the pool, is it the glass bricks underneath the former galleries? I can't stand to keep looking.

Later I'm sitting with Slawomir (again it's Agnieszka who put us in touch) in the empty breakfast room of the Hotel Pomorski, which is located outside the old town and is frequented mostly by Poles. When I ask him about the swimming pool, he tells me it wasn't until after 1989 that he learned it used to house a synagogue. Many of his friends learned to swim there, he tells me. Not him, he went to a different pool.

It's only as I'm having this conversation with Slawomir that I realize I don't know where in Offenbach, the town where I was born, the synagogue once stood. Neither before nor since '89 do I seem to have been interested in that. And now, in Poland, I'm getting indignant about the fact that the desecration of houses of worship continued after the war?

I try to excuse myself with the fact that I left my home town at fifteen and Germany at eighteen. This doesn't work; on the contrary. But hasn't that always been the case, that any outrage which erupts in me soon swings back in my face? With a burst of heat the fear flashes through my mind – pushed away almost immediately – that the public pool where I so often went swimming as a girl might also have been built in a former synagogue. I don't think it's true. But if it was? For many years I haven't asked myself this question, and now it takes only seconds for me to make sure my fear was unfounded. Unfounded? I discover that the Offenbach synagogue, after it had been set on fire and burned down from the inside in 1938, was operated as a cinema and today still serves as an 'event venue'.

I flee further into the past, to back when it was still Sanderling's present and when there were synagogues in Germany and in Poznań. One of the houses he lived in is easy to find – assuming the street numbers haven't been changed. It's located at number 3 of what used to be Wilhelmstraße, today called ulica Marcinkowskiego after a Polish physicist. It's a typical avenue, with plants in the middle and decorated with a fountain whose stone dolphins don't spit any water. Yes, the higher Prussian officials might have lived here as they presumably wished to live, that is to say, like in any other Prussian city. Did they come here to feel foreign?

Various offices and agencies are now housed in what used to be 3 Wilhelmstraße; one plaque names the trading standards office, with the Polish arms displayed resplendent above it, an eagle that resembles the Prussian eagle the way a red egg resembles a golden egg. Neither Sanderling nor anyone else lives here any longer. I wander around the Prussian quarter, essentially a town unto itself, in which there are no longer any Prussians. Massive, dismal buildings line the streets wide as boulevards, darkened by rain. I find the erstwhile Protestant church where Johannes Hesekiel preached, the pastor through whom all human filth and misery flowed as if through a purifying filter. Sanderling calls him a saint. Hanging on the walls in the vestibule of the brick church there are children's drawings of saints. The saints, like the non-saints, consist of smiley-face heads on short torsos. Over their round heads float haloes. The Protestant church hasn't been turned into a swimming pool but into a Catholic church.

How wide would the streets have to be for everything not to be far too close together? Hesekiel's church stands opposite the Collegium Maius, a hulking corner building which in those years housed the Prussian settlement commission. This organization had the task of creating a 'living rampart against the Slavic flood', that is, of driving out Poles in favour of German settlers. The people Sanderling spent time with in Posen – did he even once use the Polish name? – included, as I found out from his diary, not only Hesekiel but also Robert von Zedlitz-Trützschler, who for a time was the head of this settlement commission and later became Prussia's Culture Minister. I stand between the two buildings, between church and Prussianness, and try to imagine how goodness, the *living, clarifying stream of compassion* that seems to have emanated from Hesekiel, could have gone along with expelling Poles from their own country. They belonged together, men of the cloth, Prussian officials, their families. They were the city's good society – the best, or was there a better one still? Among the *acquaintances of intellectual nobility* from his time in Poznań, I also found in Sanderling's diary the name Alfred Knobloch. All these people, however insignificant they may seem, left traces behind that lead all the way into the great digital encyclopedia: Knobloch, who was entrusted with setting up accident insurance in agriculture, was 'an advocate of Germanization of Polish regions, as manifested among other ways in the repression of the Polish language in society and in schools'.

I've been inclined all along to regard Sanderling too as a Germanizer. Would he, who had no connection to Poland, have otherwise gone east in those years of aggressive Germanization? But recently I discovered a passage in his diary from 1891 that delighted me because it contradicts my ideas and my hasty conclusions: *Concerning the decree by the new Culture Minister, Count Zedlitz, that teachers in Polish regions will be allowed to conduct private lessons in Polish, I would like to set down the credo that has been alive in me from the beginning and that I continue to uphold, that the government has no right to take a people's language away from them and, I'd like to say, to alter the structure of the fibres of their hearts.*

If reading those lines raised my spirits, indeed, almost made me rejoice, it was because here too the straight path proved not to be straight and to break off. Laws that took effect from 1871 on were supposed to gradually 'purify' not only the territory but also the language of anything Slavic. This politics of Germanization is generally described as a precursor of the later version, as a kind of foothill of the giant mountain. And for someone who closes their eyes to individual lives and only perceives greater movements, that may be true. But the life of an individual is richer, more contradictory, less consistent than that of a society, it can't be melted together with other lives into a single trend. Sanderling is subject to those movements, that is true; like the bird whose name he bears, he's always running close to the water's edge of his time. Let's imagine a town in whose centre an announcement is due to take place, and everyone is heading in that direction. Yet among the many who make their way to that same destination, there are a few who have other thoughts as they walk, whether because the words that have been released rub them the wrong way, or because they've got something more urgent to take care of, or simply because they forgot something back at home. There won't be much about them in the history books.

I walk down ulica Kościuszki; at the next corner stands the German castle (there's also a Polish one), looking as if it has no intention of budging from that spot for the next thousand years; an ungainly, fearsome grey monstrosity, a kind of gigantic bunker with unrefined decorations. On the side facade, nearly all the windows above street level has been bricked up. A poster in front of two of the barred windows on the ground floor advertises a 'Dance Club' by the name of Bogota, which can be reached via an external staircase into the basement.

From the front, the walls are a shade lighter and I see with amazement that there's an entrance through which I can wander into the monstrosity. As behind everything old for which no particular use can any longer be found, this one hides a cultural centre. This one is called Zamek (castle). I assume that sometimes there are even visitors. Today there is at least a cashier who sells me a ticket for an exhibition of contemporary art.

First I take a look at the photos displayed in the entrance hall. They're old shots of the city centre, taken around the turn of the century, next to which you can see pictures taken from the same spots today. In the old streets there's lots of activity, vastly more than today. Even the inanimate was more animated back then: a jumble of wrought-iron embellishments, of bay windows, balconies and signs of all kinds brought movement into the facades. If one could draw a conclusion from comparing the two sets of pictures, then it would be that the past was confusion, convolutedness, curvature, the present the victory of the straight line, smoothness and emptiness.

It's only later when I'm back at the hotel that I enlarge one of the photos I took, and one of the shop signs in the background becomes legible: KAISER'S KAFFEE GESCHÄFT. Just a few decades later, that inscription will disguise the first gas vans filled with the inmates of asylums. (*Why don't you poison these people?*) In the photo, at the end of the street – ulica Święty Marcin – you can see the imperial castle. Kaiser's Kaffee Geschäft? Which Kaiser? Not the one who had this castle built, of course. More likely an entrepreneur called Kaiser. The other Kaiser's castle was later converted into a 'Führer's residence'. The longer I explore the past, the more often I see a future appearing that by now has itself long been the past. This harmless shop sign: whoever, in the first years of the century, when the picture was taken, would have imagined its story would develop as it did? The future must lie hidden in our daily surroundings in the form of a mysterious, unlearnable ideography.

The art exhibition I have a ticket for begins at the other end of the old part of the building; this allows me to penetrate inside the hulk. I'm directed towards a door. When this and another one after it close behind me, I'm alone. Marble floors, wall sconces, arcades, to the right a hall-like room with a coffered ceiling. The transformation into a residence for the Führer lasted four whole years, I read. Among other things requiring an enormous amount of both money and forced labour, the castle chapel was converted into a study, or rather vault, for the Führer.

Cultural centre? Somewhere perhaps, yes, in one tiny wing of the hulk. What I'm seeing, what I'm walking through, is a tasteless, dismal, bombastic void. It's as if I was walking alone through an emptied, desolate Louvre, eventually finding in the farthest-flung corner a junk room with the lights still on. At the end of a long arcade whose windows look out on a courtyard like something in a prison, I do then find the exhibition. A small, dark room, with a woman sitting outside on a chair, as if there would be anyone to monitor in this wasteland. The exhibition consists of retouched photos of naked people and body parts; a drooping male member on a black background, glowing like a piece of lava; a pregnant woman with her head bandaged, her belly illuminated with X-ray light. I'm glad to find my way back to the exit.

The hulk reminds me of one of those bunkers on France's Atlantic coast that can't be blown up or otherwise removed. You can neither get rid of them nor do anything with them. They're simply there, like the sea itself, and will always be there. Later in the National Museum I stand looking at *Melancholia*. Jacek Malczewski is the name of the painter, and he painted the picture in exactly the years when Sanderling lived in Poznań. In the picture, the painter sits with his back to me on the left side, at his easel. Rushing out of the canvas, hurtling into the world and towards me, are children, boys who quickly get hold of weapons – they're peasants, and their weapons are scythes not with right angles but with blades mounted straight on a long shaft – and become freedom fighters before further forward, right in front of me, they perish or else are transformed into monks or prisoners with thin hair and white beards. One of them, instead of holding a scythe, grips the neck of a violin. The men age from left to right. With the last of their strength, the old men brace themselves against the window facade on the right side of the painting, which is where this human whirlwind is determinedly heading. Behind the slightly open window there hangs, not held up by anything or anyone (nobody in this picture besides the painter himself touches the floor with their feet) and turning her back to the whirlwind, a female figure, thin, shrouded in black – melancholia? Death? A black angel of history who isn't looking backwards but at the bright and verdant green of a riverbank.

I travel to Owińska, in search of the asylum that Sanderling might in 1903 or 1904 have visited together with other pastors. And again I'm overcome with the fear that I might be doing Sanderling an injustice. Or is it his countrymen who did him an injustice in that they calmly and deliberately put into action what was the fleeting impulse of a single person, a question uttered at a time of intense anguish? In September 1939, the Germans invaded Poland. On 11 November, all the patients in the Owińska asylum were dead.

In the bus a young girl sits next to me, and what first strikes me about her is that she shows no shyness. Usually, so long as there are still pairs of empty seats remaining on a bus, new passengers who get on avoid sitting right next to someone. In this bus there are still plenty of seats free, yet this girl sits next to me, in the third or fourth row. She draws my attention a second time by intervening in a conversation between a man sitting right at the front and the driver. I don't understand what they're talking about, but it sounds as if the girl is objecting to something. The driver responds. She is persistent and again not in the least timid, following up several times.

The journey doesn't last long; Owińska is located quite near to Poznań. 'Owińska?' I say enquiringly to the girl when we approach a stop that I think could be the right one. The girl nods. Now she stands out for me a third time because she's the only passenger who gets off with me at this stop.

Right on the main street, as the bus is starting up again, there occurs between us something that, if we spoke the same language, you would call a conversation. She understands that I'm looking for what was once a convent. I understand that she's here to visit a school. She sets off at a quick pace, with me walking next to her, and we try mostly unsuccessfully to understand each other; smiling remains the only success. I don't know where to find the former Cistercian convent, which in the 1930s housed an institution that back then was still called a madhouse, but I have the feeling we, the girl and I, are heading for the same destination. And indeed the girl says goodbye to me outside the door of a building right up next to a church, a building that has to be the one I'm looking for. The church is locked. The building the girl disappeared into appears to now be a school or a care facility. Is the girl what gets called 'disabled'? Is lack of shyness a disability?

I walk round the outside of the complex of buildings, try to get into the park that lies behind it, but in vain: the garden is surrounded by railings and doesn't appear to have an entrance. I watch the joggers doing their laps inside this cage. A few days later, Anna will tell me that the convent is now a school for the blind and that nobody else is allowed into the garden. Were the joggers blind? And the girl on the bus? Presumably they see less well, or at least differently, than I do. Would they have been murdered in 1939?

I take photos of memorial plaques. Google Translate helps me decipher them. Two of the Polish directors of the hospital were, if I'm understanding correctly, deported to Dachau; only one of the two returned. As far as I can see, the murdered inmates are not memorialized. But the Polish officers and policemen who fell victim to Stalin's crimes are. The last sentence of the memorial plaque, WIECZNE ODPOCZYWANIE RACZ DAĆ IM PANIE, reads, according to the Google translation, 'Grant of eternal rest give to them Mister'. Translating may not be what computers do best; they are however sometimes good at resolving inner tensions.

I take a photo of a bedraggled NO PHOTOGRAPHY sign. Again and again the thought: What are you doing here? What do you expect to discover in these stones, railings and puddles? Under the darkening sky, I walk past mottled apartment complexes studded with round satellite dishes to an abandoned castle on the other side of the road. From the rotten windows, court ladies painted on cardboard look down at me.

It's nearly night-time when I get back to the bus stop, whose metal walls are partially missing. Someone's spray-painted a picture of the convent church on what's left of the walls, and its actual outlines can still vaguely be seen through the opening in the wall, behind some bare trees. On a board with information about the Owińska community, I look at the photograph of a body of water that must be somewhere nearby and on whose sandy beach two blonde women in bikinis lie beneath palm trees on a sun lounger and push their sunglasses up into their hair; there are tropical idylls wherever there are blonde women. In Poznań, the Germans, or rather forced labourers, had begun to create an artificial body of water by damming the Cybina river. Might this one go back to their work too? I sit down on the bench in the bus shelter and wait; the wind blows through the hole in the metal wall.

After the war (the second one), Sanderling's son, my grandfather, attempted to narrate his father's years in Poland. One chapter of the manuscript, which is called *Der Pfarrer von Połajewo* (The Pastor of Połajewo), is headed 'The Sinful Village'. If the author is to be believed, the villagers gave themselves over to the most horrible debauchery. In this place of filthy and miserable lust, vaguely human creatures lived like rabbits. That's how he describes the way the members of the Protestant community lived, though there weren't many of them; it seems unlikely that he regarded the non-Protestants as purer and more virtuous. He also recounts his father's visit, as pastor, to an asylum, yet he leaves out the passage I'm still choking on (*Why don't you poison...?*). No wonder: the mentally ill people, which included those with depression, learning difficulties and physical disabilities, have all just been poisoned by his colleagues.

He nonetheless wished to play the role of mediator, he thrust himself between his father and the world and thereby into the foreground – and am I doing anything else? One difference, though: he doesn't realize he's doing it. He means well. And me?

With some people, any meaning-well is out of place. Sanderling protrudes from those distant years, a tall spruce, a rugged crag. You might declare him insane, perhaps sneer at him. But mean him well? Can you mean well with a storm, with a smouldering volcano? *The Pastor of Połajewo* is a son's attempt to bring his father down to his level, to make him into a respectable, phoney, middle-class citizen like he himself is, I scream in my anger. I have no god to curse, no heaven to shout to. But the idea that debauchery would be considered the worst and most despicable thing by a man who made a pact with murderers, how can I forget that? How can I forget that the person who joked around morning and night with the SS men who stood guard outside his house was not at all amused by children born of lust? Then again, it's precisely because he wasn't amused by such children that I never got to know him. And that's fine with me! That's my little revenge.

The past lies before us like a path, Landauer wrote. That path is for instance the one travelled by the patients of the Owińska asylum, and so the next day I set out to look for the so-called Fort VII. Unlike the patients, I'm not transported there in a truck; I go by tram. The fort, built by the Prussians in the nineteenth century as part of the fortifications, is now situated in the middle of the city, yet it is thoroughly hidden. If the enlarged plan I printed out is correct, I must now be standing right in front of it, but I don't see anything that looks remotely like a fortification. I don't see anything except a stretch of waste ground covered with trees and bushes. That waste ground is what the young man I ask points to. And sure enough, there's a small street that turns into a path. I don't need to walk far. Heavy, glistening drops fall from rain-soaked branches, and soon I can see an elongated red-brick building, sunk into the earth all the way up to the roof, with a wide ditch opening in front of it. Above that, at some distance, a bridge leads to a gate. And with a dread I hadn't anticipated, I decipher above the gate, in broken lettering, the words KONZENTRATIONSLAGER POSEN.

What had I expected? That there would be a friendly memorial site waiting for me here, with postcards and audio guide?

I follow the path, which leads not to the large gate but to a smaller entrance off to the side. Besides the raindrops dancing on my umbrella and the distant noise of cars, I hear no sounds and don't see anyone. Although I'm otherwise not especially fearful, I feel an almost panicky anxiety as I make my way step by step inside the compound, and have to force myself not to turn around and instead to overcome the fear, which is due neither to the Germans who were once here nor the Poles who are now, nor to the memorial path lying ahead of me, newly installed, studded with wastepaper baskets and lamps and bereft of human beings, nor even to the casemates which are now decorated like chapels with flowers and candles, one of which served as a gas chamber, but rather to that inaccessible abyss, made of red stone and rutted tarmac, that hasn't changed in seventy years and is mouldering away and which is where, in front of the fortress, the raw, unprepared past abruptly jumped up at me.

'It nonetheless remains essential to evacuate every Pole who on the basis of his intellectual capability, political influence or economic power might constitute an impediment to the implementation of Deutschtum in different social circles.' There it is again, Deutschtum, now emptied of the content it once held and filled with the dead. Above the ramparts two small watchtowers. Without encountering a single human soul – encountering thousands of human souls – I walk through the basement of the Museum of the Martyrs of Greater Poland, which should include the martyrdom of the mentally ill. In the last of these vaults there sits at the entrance behind a little table a guard who briefly lifts his head as I enter: so there *is* one person apart from me in the brick caves. On a creased photo you can see the staff of the institution in Owińska, doctors and nurses, as they mark the hundred-year anniversary of the institution in 1938. A kink in the paper mutilates the face of the trombonist who sits on the ground with the other musicians in a small brass ensemble in front of the group. One of the old photos looks familiar to me. It shows a bus with opaque windows, in front of it a doctor in a white coat and a nurse invitingly holding open the door of the bus. It's a photo of Hadamar. Is something coming full circle? Is it closing outside me or around me? Is the circle carrying me away from here, to the tram and back into the city centre? Has it always been there, invisible?

A city is time petrified. I read that the gravestones from the Jewish cemetery that was destroyed in 1940/41 are scattered all around the city. In all kinds of different places: on the fairgrounds, in the paving of ulica Czartoria, on ulica Libelta, at the back of a plot of land on ulica Śniadeckich; funeral stelae, or pieces of them, have been found worked into masonry, into paving, perhaps into a bridge. In an aerial view of the fairground from the 1920s, you can still see the cemetery; if you enlarge the photo you can make out many rows of graves: hundreds of dead, over which apartment buildings now tower. And while I'm still lost in imagining this desecration of graves, another image imposes itself on me, an image of vengeance or retribution, in which the stones dispersed all over the city become containers of poison or packets of explosives that one day blow the city to smithereens, or seeds that can bloom in any corner. Without realizing it, the violators hid those stones so well in the ruins of the city that they can never again be thoroughly removed. They would have to tear down the whole city and turn over every stone to find all the gravestone fragments. And isn't this the case in every city or town in which Jewish cemeteries were razed to the ground? We inserted all those stones into our own flesh, I think, where they wander back and forth like bullets or encyst themselves.

I read that a few of these stones, scattered and found again over the course of decades, have been re-erected in ulica Głogowska, where there cemetery once was. Ulica Głogowska is many miles long; without the house number – 26a – it wouldn't be possible to find the spot. I wonder, as I approach from the fairground, where there might be room for a few gravestones on this busy street with buildings on both sides. As I get closer to number 26a, I see a woman push open the wrought-iron gate; she sees me coming, sees that I'm hurrying to slip through the door after her, and lets the gate quickly shut behind her.

For the first time, what separates me from the dead takes on the all too clear form of bars. I stand in front of those bars and look into the courtyard, where there are indeed, out of reach for me and all other passers-by, six large, new gravestones with Hebrew inscriptions, all the same, rounded at the top, black. Next to them lie four smaller pieces of stone, presumably the remains that were found. The entrance with the railings, which tapers like a telescope towards the gravestones, forms part of an ordinary, many-storeyed block of flats behind which more similar buildings can be seen. Fresh grass grows in the courtyard – deliberately sown around the new gravestones? Behind me, a tram rumbles past, and the noise of the city warms my back.

Next day I stand in front of bars for the second time when I enter the Holy Blood Church on ulica Żydowska. The Holy Blood Church was built on the spot where, in 1399, communion bread was found that had allegedly been desecrated by Jews. Centuries later, a table was discovered in a house in the same street, bricked up inside a pillar. And it was adjudged that the desecrated host must have been skewered on this table. In a solemn procession, the table was carried into the neighbouring church. I read about this and was prepared to find said table in a corner of the church as proof of the desecration, or as proof of the deep-seated belief in it, but the interior of the church is closed. I'm standing in front of railings through which I can see into the dark church but without being able to make anything out; only all the way back in the apse is there a light on. Whether a table and the host are stored somewhere here, I don't know. Clutching a bar in each hand, I look into the darkness. Haven't I lost sight of Sanderling too much since I've been in Poland? What does he have to do with this church and its walled-in table? Have I read even one anti-Semitic remark from him in all the notes and writings I've got hold of? As always when such thoughts occur to me, I bring out

Buber, Benjamin, Gutkind, Scholem, Rosenzweig and set them up as a shield around my great-grandfather. All those friendships began after he had returned to the West. From reading his notes, you might think there were no Jews at all in Poland, and only a handful of Catholics. As if the Germans lived among themselves, the way colonial masters all around the world typically did. And yet most of the big shops on the town hall square were owned by Jews, and there were Jewish doctors and lawyers in Poznań. I imagine that, more or less out of necessity, the townsfolk encountered other kinds of people in day-to-day life, but preferred to socialize with those of the same religion.

The town hall square is not far from the Holy Blood Church. There are no shops there any more, and certainly no Jewish ones. Only restaurants and bars and a tourist information centre. The town hall is no longer a town hall but a museum of city history. Maybe here I'll get closer to the past? The captions are in Polish.

On the top floor, placed in the middle of a room, is a large model of the synagogue. I have Google translate the long Polish texts and find out that the building could house 1,200 people, that it was thus enormous, that the dome is reminiscent of a Byzantine basilica and that the interior is richly decorated. The translation swings back and forth, as I do during these days, between present and past, as if the ornamentation of this dome and these wall decorations still existed, as if they hadn't long ago given way to the blue tiles of a swimming pool. The model takes up a lot of room, even protruding slightly over the edge of its podium. There's no mention at all of the later history of the building. I don't rule out the possibility that because of my lack of knowledge of Polish I have overlooked something, but I don't believe so. For in general the history of Poznań's Jews doesn't appear to be part of the city's history. The only testimony of it I discover, besides the model of the synagogue, is a small oil painting depicting a few crooked gravestones in an old Jewish cemetery.

Then I look at a school report card from the Poznań Pestalozzi School from 1905, the year of the big school strike, which I know was a response to the Prussian ban on teaching Polish and the order to attend religious lessons in German. In 1905 there were twice as many Polish as German pupils in Poznań province; nonetheless, you were only allowed to speak German. Polish parents and children resisted, refusing to attend lessons. In the report, one young pupil, Franziska Slorna, is charged with having refused to answer in religion class. The only good mark Franziska has is in gymnastics, where she was permitted not to speak German. Two caricatures show a Prussian policeman with moustache, spiked helmet and thrust-out chest over a tightly belted belly. Next to him a small child, being led away in chains.

The measures aimed to bring about Germanization brought about the opposite. The more the Germans insisted on their Deutschtum, the more the Poles stuck to their Polishness. They avoided the Germans, and boycotted their shops. Polish children now only received as gifts dolls dressed in traditional Polish costume, and under no circumstances the ugly, heavy lead soldiers with the spiked helmet, instead Hussars.

In an 1859 oil painting of the city, Poznań resembles a small flat Flemish town with cows grazing on broad meadows. There are already Prussian policemen walking back and forth in front of the city walls, even if they are substantially thinner than the ones in the later caricatures, and between them is a gentleman with top hat and mutton chops.

At the start of the following century, as the situation – his own inner state, but also that between Germans and Poles – intensified, Sanderling was a pastor in Połajewo (pronounced Pouayevo). I plan to travel to this village, fifty kilometres or so north of Poznań, the next morning, as if there might still be traces there of his distress, his struggle to reach a more and more remote and incomprehensible God. There's a bus to Połajewo, but I almost abandon my plan before I've even left the bus station: the woman at the counter doesn't understand me, or at least acts as if she doesn't. Because even place names must be declined, you in effect need to speak Polish to buy a ticket. The woman shrugs and looks at the next person in the queue. Finally a girl who speaks English helps me. Ticket in hand, I wait for the bus. In the bus station toilets, a woman whom in France we would call Dame Pipi approaches me as I'm leaving. To give me change, she tips into my hand the few coins that were in her saucer. I have the impression that she lives in the little room next to the toilets, in this loud calm place where a constant coming and going reigns. She laughs.

The bus drives a long way through suburban areas, then after a while we're on flat land, as flat as in the painting in the museum; after an hour and a half I get out. I'm in Połajewo. Two other passengers get out, and they both quickly go on their way. I stand by the side of the road, see myself standing there as if in a well-known movie scene that will continue like this: while I stand there, the bus will drive off again and, on the other side of the street, right opposite me, someone will be looking at me: Sanderling.

There's nobody standing on the other side. Next to me, two women are raking up dead leaves on a long strip of lawn, each of them with a rake, without the noisy blowers that get used where I'm from. The bus has vanished; I'm all alone in Połajewo and can only hope that at some point it will turn round and take me back. A slight feeling of trepidation gives way to an urge to laugh: I made it! Now I'm here. As if it had been particularly difficult. Or is the difficulty perhaps still to come?

The women briefly raise their heads as I walk past them. I try to appear as local as possible, but my efforts are in vain: not only because they don't succeed, but also and above all because – to my relief – my presence draws little attention. The bus stopped between two churches that are only a few paces, let's say two hundred, away from each other, one of them bright and trim, the other dreary and run-down. I turn to the latter. It's the kind of brick church you see all over northern Germany, presumably the former Protestant church. It's lost part of its spire. The way it stands there, maimed, by the side of the road, it resembles the two recently pruned trees outside its front facade, which dumbly stretch their branch-stumps towards the sky. There's no glass left in the windows; the steps outside the entrance are overgrown with weeds. And already in these first moments, looking at these helpless stumps, I have to think of the small man with the great longing for more, for something different and higher, of my godforsaken great-grandfather with his fists clenched, screaming *swine* and *scoundrel* at heaven. This church is where he stood and preached, for far too long, probably, and far too intensely for the small German congregation who had squeezed together in the front rows of the half-empty church and stared at him, at first taken aback, then severe, then colder and colder in the face of so much agitation and fervour. He looked into the curious, indifferent faces like someone who despaired of being able to bring a dead person back to life.

Thanks to Google Street View, I already saw the church on my screen before my departure. There was a sign in front saying, in Polish, FOR SALE. Later, back in Poznań, Slawomir will tell me that in the meantime the church has been sold. To a former policeman who wants to convert it into – a cultural centre.

I haven't got far from the bus when my eye falls on a building that could just as well house the police or the village administration and which I only notice because a man is stepping out of the door and holds it wide open for a moment while he exchanges a few words with a woman in the lobby. On the sign next to the entrance I read BIBLIOTEKA PUBLICZNA. And the thought occurs to me: if there's someone in this village who might be able to give you information – but about what exactly? what is it you want to know? – then this is where they'll be. This is the home of books and of the past, this is where they get read and it gets looked after.

I step inside. The woman behind the reception desk greets me in a friendly manner, *dzień dobry*, and that emboldens me, but how will things go from here? I take from my pocket the sheet of paper I have at the ready for all situations and try to pronounce the Polish phrases listed there, which despite my efforts don't exactly sound Polish in my mouth. I end up simply handing the woman the piece of paper, the way profoundly deaf or foreign people do in the metro to make themselves understood. I point to the sentences about Sanderling and Połajewo (there are other things on the already very creased sheet: *Kawa, proszę*, coffee, please, and *Gdzie jest dworzec kolejowy?* Where is the railway station?). I also present a photo that I think shows the former parsonage.

She smiles. Haven't I almost reached my goal? Was my goal perhaps to test the animosity of Polish people towards Germans? Clearly I was counting on greater animosity: every friendly smile feels to me like a victory.

Then I realize the woman assumes I'm French, because there are phrases in French and Polish on the sheet. She phones to ask one of her colleagues to come, a woman who is in exceedingly good spirits and endearing and who remains that way even in light of my Germanness. She speaks a little French and English and immediately knows of someone who can help me. (So someone can help me!) She telephones one of, no, *the* local historian, who's ready to drop everything and come to us where we are in the library. While we're waiting she invites me up to the second floor, into the office of the director, who only speaks Polish but who smiles in a no less friendly manner than her colleagues and will, during the whole conversation, sit behind her huge desk and benevolently follow what's happening. We animatedly try to make ourselves understood to each other while drinking instant coffee. It might even be happiness, what I feel during these moments with these unfamiliar people in this foreign land. Is that possible? A happy German in Poland? I prefer not to imagine the derisive chuckles this idea would provoke in Stasiuk.

Through the window we see the man who was summoned hurrying over. Yes, he's interested, look at him run, says the library employee with a laugh.

The local historian is a lively older gentleman, retired presumably, and he seems to be well acquainted with both the librarians, one of whom translates for him as best she can. He wrote a book with the title *Moje Połajewo*, My Połajewo, which I'd like to own so it might perhaps become *my* Połajewo; they insist on giving me a copy. As they show me right away, it contains a short chapter about the Protestant community, in which the Protestant townspeople are listed by name, and sure enough among them is (under his real name) Sanderling. There's also a photograph of the former parsonage, though it bears no resemblance to the grand villa in the photo I have (which is one I took of a photo at my father's). Who knows where that villa might be located? In any case, it's not in this village, the local historian is sure about that. The actual parsonage is diagonally opposite the library and can be seen from its windows. It's a simple, unplastered one-storey house whose only notable feature is that it boasts, under the eaves, between the main floor and the attic, a row of small, square window openings. In general it looks to me as if it dates from the 1940s, in any case certainly not from Sanderling's time, and the 1940s is the period the historian tells me about when I ask how the Protestants, Catholics and Jews lived here together in the past. It was peaceful, they all got along well with one another, he says. According to what the historian's mother told him, the pastor, Father Hoppe, always used to take walks with the Catholic priest, and the two of them had amicable conversations. (At this point there's a misunderstanding that prompts lots of amusement, because at first I thought Father Hoppe liked to take walks with the historian's mother.) Then later Father Hoppe joined the NSDAP. At that time you had to do so, he tells me. But he was a good man, he says. I ask about the local Jewish community. I'm told there were ten Jewish families in the village. Ten families, I think; that's about a hundred people. I don't ask what became of them. Their names are listed in *Moje Połajewo*. (Later, once I'm back home, Agnieszka will translate various parts of the book. There was a synagogue in the village, she reads, which fell into ruin and was demolished in the late 1930s. Ruined and demolished in the late 1930s? The synagogue was destroyed and the Jews were killed, I say, but Agnieszka finds my deduction premature. Perhaps this is a difference between Germans and other people: the latter can't believe what happened, they have a moment of hesitation in which they wonder if it really can be true. They believe you shouldn't always think the worst. That same day Agnieszka also tells me that when she went to school in Poland in the 1980s, she went on a school trip to Auschwitz and that no particular mention was made of Jews. She also tells me about her grandfather, who always maintained firmly and rigidly that in 1939 Poland was invaded not only by the Germans but also by the Soviets. As children, she and her brother regarded the old man as a bit meschugge. She tells me they believed their schoolbooks, and in those there was only a German invasion.) – So he was a good man, this Father Hoppe. But he can't have gone for walks with the rabbi, since he had by that time probably already been murdered. I think this without saying it. Have I, the progeny of Germans, perhaps come here to reproach the Poles for not having taken walks with their rabbis?

The historian offers to look in the local archive in the next few days for documents that might relate to Sanderling, and to send me copies. When we talk about the mountains of files stored in German archives, this person who all along has been speaking only Polish and obviously knows no German at all, says, right in the middle of a sentence in Polish, the words '*Ordnung muss sein*'. Everyone laughs good-naturedly, even the director behind her desk; even I do. I'll tell Anna about this the next day, and she will explain to me that the words '*Ordnung muss sein*' are in general use and have entered the Polish language, as 'Wunderkind' or 'Mamma mia' have entered English, I presume. As I did this time, I always laugh along when in Poland, France or wherever else; people laugh at the Germans, usually in a surprisingly unmalicious way. This laughter does me good. So our national characteristics, or what are taken for them – orderliness, punctuality – can be greeted with smiles, I think. Our meticulousness can be seen with something besides horror, our conscientiousness not as lack of conscience but as an endearing mania. *Our*? Am I part of that group? Still? Even though I've remained away from the country for so long? Do I carry the country around with me, along with its language, its history and its other component parts, some of which are reflected by the clichés? Is my country part of my genetic inheritance? I think so. Maybe I would have had a chance to escape it if as a newborn I'd been adopted by a family from Papua New Guinea. As it is... *Ordnung muss sein*. Haven't

I always made an honest effort to be disorderly, unpunctual, unmeticulous and under no circumstances obstinate and rigid? With so much success that I got the nickname 'Panzerdivision'.

Later I find myself standing in the village looking at the bare moonscape of a chicken yard strewn with craters, boulders and old car tyres. Two dozen hens turn their pursed rear ends towards me. I try to imagine Połajewo over a hundred years ago, in November, in February, in May. A few loamy paths, one broader track that cuts right through the village, past the two churches, and then it's up and away, towards more comfort, to running water and electricity, brilliant society and piano music. But there is a world whose centre is Połajewo. Around Połajewo there are twenty or so smaller villages or estates that can be reached on foot in two or three hours and to which Sanderling regularly walks, since he is accountable to God for the scattered souls of the Protestants. He could live somewhere else altogether, in the Taunus mountains, for instance, or the hillsides above the Rhine, where his descendants will later make themselves at home. He had ahead of him what is commonly called a 'glittering career in administration', but even without that he could have allowed himself a comfortable life, wherever he wished to. But he prefers to allow himself an uncomfortable life in Połajewo. He isn't happy here, and is less and less so. Soon he'll be forty years old, yet his ideals have lost nothing of their unsatisfiability. One of those is *to elevate the plain countryside*. This might sound like something within a human's power. But what he means by it is about as futile as if he had resolved to literally hoist up the plain countryside by a hundred metres. He imagines the villagers of the future as people *who can handle manure even as their personalities are steeped in acute spiritual penetration*, whose *soul capacity* would embrace metaphysical and physical life and *represent it in action*. He's thinking here not only of individuals, rather he wishes to make the whole village *the birthplace of a breed of people*. A new kind of person who in their inner faith would resemble Saint Francis and would thus know how to manage their farm shrewdly and progressively. The old breed of people Sanderling discovers in Połajewo are characterized more by obtuseness and stubbornness – he calls it *swampy stagnation* – but fine, if everything were already perfect you wouldn't need to take the trouble. He has set himself a goal and gets to work. He begins with school lessons, for which as pastor he is responsible, delves into the current teaching methods and, no surprise here, agrees with none of them. For in his eyes, learning reading, writing and arithmetic shouldn't be a formal matter. He begins from the notion that a child who, for instance, learns the word 'mouse' should at the same time be taught not simply about the life and mores of mice, but must take the step *from the low individual to the high general*, and finally to the highest of all general things, God, and thereby to the whole of Christian teaching. According to Sanderling's method, which presumably wasn't put into practice anywhere besides this village and by him personally, a child who learns how to write 'mouse' also likewise learns everything beyond that. And isn't he correct? Doesn't every mouse indeed contain the whole universe? And isn't it the task of the teacher to extract the universe from the mouse?

He doesn't get far with his method. Far and wide, there's nobody for whom, as for him, the misery, the outer and inner poverty of these people out in the country, is *a bitter tribulation*. He exerts himself in vain. He is alone.

In Połajewo there's an old weeping willow in front of the Catholic church. Out of reach, in a cavity in the hefty trunk, garlanded with radiant, flourishing shoots of willow, is a small Virgin Mary, behind white plastic lilies and roses, her head leaning slightly to one side, praying.

Sanderling did not, he found, resemble a tree with wide branches and a radial root system, but rather the slender spruce that instead of striving horizontally strives vertically, towards heaven, so as to drive its single taproot more deeply into the earth. Seen from my distant vantage point, there's nothing he less resembles than a tree. He's always in motion; a small, energetic figure charging purposefully and using the utmost energy now in this, now in that direction, running into walls, recoiling before the abyss at the last minute, turning back. Also doing the opposite, wrong thing. He's someone who never stands still. His life is, as few lives have ever been, made up from his first breath to his last of turning points, crises and about-faces. This time, however, in Połajewo, it's about the whole thing. In reality it's always about the whole thing, with the word 'mouse' as with any other word; for him, it's always about far more than a word, than a human being, even the strongest-willed, even he, can bear. For him it's about more than life and death.

Here, in front of the weeping willow, where he himself might have stood more than a hundred years ago, I commemorate him with fervour; his absoluteness, his severe nature, his boundless seriousness, his uncomfortableness and restlessness. His desperation.

The German verb gedenken (to commemorate) mostly occurs, according to computer statistics, in connection with the following terms: victim, minute's silence, anniversary, National Socialism, war victim, world war, Jew. The word deutsch (German) in connection with bank, Telekom, Bahn, economy, post, Bundestag, championship, stock exchange.

Poznań, where the bus has finally returned me, is where in December 1939 Himmler watched people with learning disabilities being gassed 'in the company of invited guests'. And once more, perhaps one last time during this journey through time, a resistance rears up inside me to the idea of a short circuit leading from Sanderling to his son and which in the end rests on a single piece of evidence. No, I don't accept that linking of the generations. In my hotel room, a few metres away from the spot where Himmler praised his people for having murdered countless men, women and children, and having stacked them up in piles while always remaining *decent*, I arrive at the conclusion, which is not in fact a conclusion but merely a beginning, that all the explanations I've read up to now – about how one generation is supposed to have brought forth another, based on Darwinism, anti-Semitism, the dwindling of God, et cetera – pertain to something that doesn't exist, or only as a mental construct, the state of mind of the masses, and that in reality there are only individuals with their individual attitudes or lack of attitudes, and within those individuals, or in most of them, the quiet or droning voices of their conscience. Books have it wrong, there aren't any masses, there are only a father and a son or a mother and a daughter, and between them are paths that lead further or break off. The explanations in books don't explain the lives and thoughts and actions of those individuals.

Why don't you kill these people?

Because I'm not a murderer.

I can't prove it, but I sense that the thought imposing itself upon me gets at something correct: the father, Sanderling, himself at times close to madness, could think and pose a question like that, and could as he said it also mean it seriously – not taking something seriously was not an option available to him – but what the question demanded is something he would never have done, and would also not have wanted others to do. The son on the other hand would never have uttered that question; he even censored it. 'In the realms of poverty of imagination,' writes Karl Kraus, 'that which is not thought must be carried out.' He didn't think it, but he did it. Not by his hand, naturally; first-hand he wrote 'reports'. He did it by making a pact with the ones who did it.

The next day is All Saints' Day, which in Poland is combined with All Souls' Day into a massive festival of the holy and unholy dead. In their honour, the living are up and about bright and early; from my window I see them carrying through the alleys their plastic bags filled with grave decorations and garden implements. Bagless, I join them. I remember reading that in 1934 in Germany, and thus shortly afterwards in Poznań, the Day of the Dead was abolished as a public holiday. To some extent the dead themselves were to be abolished. The same people who killed more people than anyone ever had before didn't want to hear or see anything of the dead. The dead, not only the ones they murdered, were to be banished forever from people's memories. Poznań's cemeteries – Jewish, of course, but also Catholic and Protestant – were expropriated under German rule and more than a few of them quickly flattened, with the remaining Catholic cemeteries being closed to visitors.

I want to go to Miłostowo, the large cemetery on the outskirts of town, but I don't want to ask anyone for directions, don't want to expose myself as someone who has neither a plastic bag nor a dead relative. Because of construction, the trams are taking different routes from those shown on the map, so I take a taxi, and soon I'm sitting silently behind a silent driver, wedged in among thousands of cars crawling forward on a four-lane street that leads east. Inert faces move past us unspeakably slowly, some of which, after a gentle struggle, we leave behind us, while others catch up, silent and stubborn like snails, faces level with mine, a huge four-row chain of animated dwellings. On the back seats, piles of bags for the cemetery.

The living are sitting in traffic on their way to the dead.

Inescapably I find myself caught up in their stream, they pull me along with them, slowly, infinitely slowly, in a tempo that leaves me plenty of time to recognize the symbol of which I'm one part, creeping along heading out of the city: a symbol of life that shows us how we hobblingly, each in our own capsule, make our way towards death.

Near the end of the drive we pass miles of cars parked by the side of the road. I get out. And I'm immediately once again taken up by a mass movement, by the wide current in which the people getting out of the trams that slide up one after the other join together with those getting out of cars and those who came on foot, past stands peddling flowers both artificial and natural, candles and lanterns of all shapes and sizes, gingerbread hearts and other baked goods. Most of those making their way forward have already stocked up; for the supermarkets, the death business is a foretaste of Christmas business. Nobody is hurrying. The whole day and the whole evening belong to the dead. Pushchairs are wheeled carefully through the crowd, with the bigger children held by the hand so they don't get submerged. A relaxed, even merry mood is in the air; nobody is wearing a mournful expression. As outside football stadiums or concert halls, metal barriers are supposed to funnel the stream which, with me in its midst, now goes into and up out of the other side of an underpass and into the woods, where it splits in two, yet the two streams don't lose each other: the parallel streams come back together, roll on until they cover the land of the dead like a broad web languidly spreading itself out.

I watch as the living separate themselves from the mass in small clusters, how they unerringly make their way towards the gravestones that belong to them and without either rushing or pausing set to work pruning ivy, tearing out weeds, cleaning off the border around the grave with the small brush they've brought along and finally distributing the new plants and candles. Only then do they stand up and form a semicircle before their dead. With their eyes focused on the grave, they quietly exchange a few words. Are the dead present in this relaxed murmuring or anywhere else? Does someone call them on the day of the dead?

There are now more living than dead in Miłostowo cemetery. I'm in among them, standing in front of a little girl's grave and thinking about a story I read in the work of Mickiewicz, in his great verse drama *Forefathers' Eve*, which, I gathered from Agnieszka, everyone in Poland knows: two dead children appear at the meal dedicated to them at the festival of the dead. 'What do you need, little soul, to enter heaven?' the living ask one of the children. 'Do you have a longing for the glory of God? Or perhaps for some candy?' – 'Nothing, we don't need anything at all,' replies the child. 'Our time on earth was splendid;

from morning to night we ran through the meadows, plucked flowers and picked fruit, singing all the while. Our short life was sweet, nothing darkened it; that's why we're unhappy now. We didn't appear for the prayers, nor for a banquet, not for the mass nor for the Christmas cookies. But you could do us one favour: we'd really like two peppercorns.'

And without my willing it or really understanding it, my thoughts form a bridge between those two peppercorns, which embody a touching minimum of bitterness and sharpness, and the most extreme evil that human beings have experienced, and to a sentence in a book of interviews with H.G. Adler, which I remember only approximately. This sentence, which I barely dare to repeat, that's how unbelievable it appears to me, says more or less that he doesn't regret anything he's experienced, even if he regrets that something like that – 'an Auschwitz', he says, I think – took place; but since such a thing did exist, then he, Adler, doesn't regret having been there.

It seems to me that such a sentence could never have been uttered and that I therefore could never have read it. And yet I'm sure I did.

Now I'm standing in front of the tomb of an unknown person. Someone, in a makeshift way, has moved the withered leaves from the mound of earth, on which there's no stone or even a wooden stone to indicate that this is a grave, and decorated it with two fir branches, an aster and a tea light. Today, then, it's not just that everyone is celebrating their ancestors, but that the strangers and the nameless are also being commemorated, those whom nobody remembers any more and who can only be conveyed into the present, made present, as a faceless, unnamed mass, an army of shadows. An army of Catholic shadows. Or do the Poles also commemorate the non-Catholics?

I wander for a long time through the cemetery wood, which is criss-crossed by a pulsating maze of paths, part of a powerful, murmuring organism that knows nothing of its own individual cells. I see thousands of the living walking over thousands of the dead. And all at once the ground is no longer a dull surface but a mirror in which we see the future reflected.

When I leave the cemetery it's already afternoon, but the festival of the dead has only just begun. I take a tram back into town to make my way to the small Jeżycki Cemetery, which is situated not far from the former concentration camp and which had been particularly recommended by Anna's husband, a lover of cemeteries. More gingerbread hearts, candles, flowers, new throngs of people, in a smaller space. Here too nobody takes any notice of me, preoccupied as they all are with tidying up and looking at their graves. I feel like an invisible visitor, deader than the dead.

It's still broad daylight, yet the candles are already burning; hundreds, thousands of lights, which will be lit up little by little by the falling night. The people have now nearly all stopped moving, and they stand in silence or quietly exchanging words in front of the gravestones and don't look as if they're waiting for something. They stand there, each in their own hereditary spot, and spend the afternoon in the company of their dead.

One young girl made of stone sits and leans her weathered head on her open hand. In the crook of the other arm, which peeks out of a little short-sleeved dress, there lies a rose, in full bloom, blazing red and shining against the grey stone, its soft petals opened as if in a cry of life.

Church bells ring. Hardly anyone stirs. Along with the few people who do tear themselves away from the graves, I move towards the cemetery chapel, a large, modern church outside which the faithful for whom there's no room left inside congregate like statues. Mass has begun. Driven by the urgent wish to leave behind, at least for a short time, this external realm where I've been stuck since the first day of my trip and perhaps since the first day of my life, I force myself into the full church, where the priest's dark voice crackles over the loudspeakers. It also stretches out over the cemetery. I stand there, held in place by the silent crowd, and close my eyes, listening to the impenetrable speech, which I gradually do partially understand, something that seems to be coming less from the priest's mouth than from his throat, something which in Polish might well be identical with soul, certainly from the depths of his chest. Something that can't be translated into any language and yet is language, chiefly consonants, transmitted into the church vault by the vibrating vocal chords of the for me invisible priest, and in or along with those sounds there resonates something else, something I can barely identify and to which I give the name 'vibrato of the dead'.

I, the heathen, make the gestures of piety along with the others, and quietly join in the murmuring. With wonder, I hear unfamiliar, meaningless sounds cross my lips. Isn't this blasphemy? I ask myself. But no. I think about the phrase 'speaking in tongues'.

Then the congregation kneels down; those who found places on the pews sink down onto the kneelers, those behind them onto the stone floor. With my head lowered and my eyes closed, I kneel in their midst and feel my scepticism and coolness wrestling with the faith that surrounds me. I don't know how much time passes. Shoulder to shoulder, we stand up, and I don't care any more how the struggle ended or whether I'm ridiculous, I just know that the voice is still vibrating up above us, a vocalized soul bereft of comprehensible meaning. And for a second time, we fall onto our knees and fold our hands, as people do. And I do it too, yes, I pray, if prayer is an extreme stretching and reaching towards something seen or suspected, if it is outer motionlessness and the greatest possible inner movement; if so, then I'm praying, kneeling in the throng, before the grey mound of earth of the unknown person and praying, I fill up the nameless grave with my dead, with those who've disappeared into the earth or wherever; I try, exerting myself as much as I'm capable of, to tear them from nothingness. I lay Sanderling, the ancestor, to rest, along with his unworthy son, my grandfather, and finally also his son, who's still standing on the edge of the abyss and has been for years. Behind my closed eyelids, my ancestors don't remain alone for long; others whose faces I don't recognize push their way forward, light, blurred figures who become more and more numerous, yet there's still room in the grave, it gets bigger and bigger, until it takes on dimensions that can't be grasped with the eye or with the mind. Until it encompasses all of them, the millions and millions of dead. My forebears.

A leg brushes against my shoulder, the organ drones to signal it's time to leave; I hurry to stand up. Dazed as if woken from a deep sleep, I see the procession of priests and choirboys gliding between the rows of pews towards the exit, clouded in incense, and now, as I slowly return from the world of images to the world of thoughts, I take fright at my all-encompassing prayer, and out of fear and shame I'm tempted to recant it all. For I hear voices sending me back to my place, at my ancestors' side. The voices say: 'Our dead don't belong to you'; they say: 'Your forebears! Such presumption!' They are the voices of those who have many dead and no grave. I have no answer. Or do I?

Are the living, then, a mirror of the dead for all time? Do they break down into the same two halves as their ancestors, into one half that perpetrated crimes or let them happen and another that suffered them? Is that my inheritance, an eternal curse?

The procession carries me out of the cemetery, where the people stand, unchanged, before their graves in the gathering dusk and don't move as the procession passes down the alleys, just turn slightly so as not to show their backs to the wooden cross that is being carried through the cemetery. In the twilight, above the glimmering of the candles which grows more and more lively, the cloudy sky has taken on a blue colour.

But the day is not yet over, the dead aren't ready for it to end, they want to have company until late into the night, and the living haven't yet tired of their company. And although I'm frozen through and exhausted, I feel myself drawn once more to the other end of the city, to the cemetery in the woods. By now I know the routes and trams that lead from one cemetery, or cmentarz, to the other. Once I reach Miłostowo it's night, but stretching out above the cemetery woods, visible already from afar, is a reddish glow.

Along with night, silence falls on the many who at this hour are still walking around. Once more I make my way through the frontier of the underpass and dive into the woods of the dead with other quiet people until we reach the first clearing. What I now behold takes my breath away, almost my sight too; I walk silently and marvel, as if I were walking through a starry sky; 'field of stars' is the term that comes to mind. There's no illumination here besides the countless wax and oil lights spread out over the graves, flickering in the deep of the wooded night, a calm, sustained fireworks display, ignited by the living for the dead.

Among the people walking through these fields of light and talking with one another, there's nobody who doesn't talk in a subdued voice that can only be heard by the person right next to them, even the children, some of whom carry buzzing filaments through the darkness, so that it might seem to someone wandering through the cemetery as if since the morning a reversal had taken place or as if they could see everything differently, namely those quietly running around as the dead, or spirits awoken to short midnight lives, and the bright flickering lights as the living.

I plunge back into the woods, walk, accompanied by the distant ghost voices, through deepest darkness, until a new clearing of light opens up and then the woods enfold me again, and so I penetrate deeper and deeper into the funereal forest of the living, intermingled with islands of light, and, making my way past these locks of light one after the other, I approach the hope that somewhere in these depths of light and shadow there might be a place where all the dead, undivided, are my, our, forebears.

REFERENCES, SOURCES, NOTES

SOME OF THE TEXTS REFERRED TO IN *SANDERLING*

In order of mention:

H.G. Adler, *Der verwaltete Mensch* (The Administered Man), Mohr, 1974

Die geschlechtlichsittlichen Verhältnisse der evangelischen Landbewohner im Deutschen Reiche (The Sexual and Moral Conditions of Protestant Country Dwellers in the German Empire), Reinhold Werther, 1896

Moritz Jaffé, *Die Stadt Posen unter preußischer Herrschaft* (The City of Poznań under Prussian Rule), Duncker & Humblot, 1909

Otto Dov Kulka, *Landscapes of the Metropolis of Death*, trans. Ralph Mandel, Harvard University Press, 2013

Andrzej Stasiuk, *Dojczland* (Germany), Suhrkamp, 2008

Czesław Miłosz, *The Captive Mind*, Knopf, 1953

Ewa Czerwiakowski and Angela Martin, eds, *Muster des Erinnerns: Polnische Frauen als KZ-Häftlinge in einer Tarnfabrik von Bosch* (Patterns of Memory: Polish Women Prisoners of a Concentration Camp Disguised as a Bosch Factory), Metropol, 2005

Gustav Landauer, *Die Revolution*, Rütten & Loening, 1907

Walter Benjamin, *Gesammelte Briefe* (Collected Letters), Suhrkamp, 2000; a comparable English edition was published by the University of Chicago Press in 1994

Richard Faber and Christine Holste, eds, *Der Potsdamer Forte-Kreis: Eine utopische Intellektuellenassoziation zur europäischen Friedenssicherung* (The Potsdam Forte Circle: A Utopian Intellectual Association for European Peacekeeping), Königshausen & Neumann, 2001

Martin Buber, *Das dialogische Prinzip* (The Dialogic Principle), Lambert Schneider, 1962; for a similar English version see Martin Buber, *Between Man and Man*, Martino Fine Books, 2014

Meister Eckhart, *Mystische Schriften: Aus dem Mittelhochdeutschen und mit einem Nachwort von Gustav Landauer* (Mystical Writings: Translated from Middle High German and with an Afterword by Gustav Landauer), Insel, 1991

Ernst Klee, *'Euthanasie' im Dritten Reich: Die 'Vernichtung lebensunwerten Lebens'* ('Euthanasia' in the Third Reich: The 'Destruction of Life Unworthy of Life'), Fischer, 1999

Gregor Dotzauer, 'Mann ohne Mitte' (Man without a Centre), *Tagesspiegel*, 2015

Max Scheler, *Die Ursachen des Deutschenhasses* (The Causes of Germanophobia), Kurt Wolff, 1917

Matthias Claudius, *Sämtliche Werke* (Complete Works), Artemis & Winkler, 1995

Walter Benjamin, *Über den Begriff der Geschichte* (On the Concept of History), in *Gesammelte Werke* (Collected Works), ed. Hermann Schweppenhäuser und Rolf Tiedemann, vol. I/2, Suhrkamp, 1991

Raul Hilberg, *The Destruction of the European Jews*, revised edition, Holmes & Meier, 1985

Karl Kraus, 'In dieser großen Zeit' (In This Great Time), *Die Fackel* no. 404, 5 December 1914

Adam Mickiewicz, *Forefathers' Eve*, trans. Charles S. Kraszewski, Glagoslav, 2016

H.G. Adler, *Der Wahrheit verpflichtet: Interviews, Gedichte, Essays* (Committed to the Truth: Interviews, Poems, Essays), Bleicher, 1998

Transforming a manuscript into the book
you hold in your hands is a group project.

Anne would like to thank everyone
who helped to publish *Sanderling*.

THE INDIGO PRESS TEAM

Susie Nicklin
Phoebe Barker
Phoebe Evans

JACKET DESIGN

Luke Bird

PUBLICITY

Sophie Portas

EDITORIAL PRODUCTION

Tetragon

COPY-EDITOR

Sarah Terry

PROOFREADER

Alexander Middleton

And especially Neil Blackadder, who translated it marvellously.

I

THE
INDIGO
PRESS

The Indigo Press is an independent publisher of contemporary fiction and non-fiction, based in London. Guided by a spirit of internationalism, feminism and social justice, we publish books to make readers see the world afresh, question their behaviour and beliefs, and imagine a better future.

Browse our books and sign up to our newsletter for special offers and discounts:

theindigopress.com

Follow *The Indigo Press* on social media for the latest news, events and more:

⊗ @PressIndigoThe
◉ @TheIndigoPress
ⓕ @TheIndigoPress
▣ The Indigo Press
♪ @theindigopress